Other books by this author:

Dedicated to Amina and Timmy

Level 5

Leadership and Management in Health and Social Care and Children and Young Peoples' Services

The down-to-earth learner support guide

S.K. Porter-Brooks

Contents

Introduction 14

Chapter 1: Communication 16

    Why is Communication Important? 16

    How to Promote Effective communication 22

    Barriers and Challenges to Communication 25

    Legal and Ethical Tensions Regarding Confidentiality and Sharing Information 30

    Information-sharing Protocols and Principles 32

    GDPR 33

Chapter 2: Promoting Professional Development........................36

    The Importance of Continually Improving Knowledge and Practice 36

    Pros and Cons of Different Methods and Approaches for Supporting Professional Development....................................40

    How to Weigh up and Decide on Different Approaches towards Continuous Professional Development.....................43

    Models of Reflective Practice 44

    Kolb's Learning Cycle 45

    Gibb's Reflective Cycle 47

Johns' Model for Structured Reflection 48

   Explain the importance of reflective practice to improve performance..49

Chapter 3: Championing Equality, Diversity and Inclusion 52

   Models of Practice that Underpin Equality, Diversity and Inclusion 52

   Potential Effects of Barriers to Equality and Inclusion 53

   The Impact of Legislation and Policy Initiatives 55

   How to Promote Equality, Diversity and Inclusion..................58

   Interventions can Both Promote Equality and Inclusion: or Reinforce Discrimination and Exclusion 61

   Effectiveness of Systems and Processes in Promoting Equality, Diversity and Inclusion 63

   Ethical Dilemmas: Balancing Rights and Duty of Care.............65

   The Concept of Informed Choice...66

   How Issues affecting Mental Capacity can Influence Informed Choice..67

Chapter 4: Promoting Health and Safety 69

   The Legislative Framework for Health, Safety and Risk Management..69

Maintaining and Helping Others to Sustain a Balanced Approach to Risk Management 74

Chapter 5: Work in Partnership in Health and Social Care 77

Features of Partnership Working 77

Partnership Working: with Colleagues; Other Professionals; Others 80

Chapter 6: Lead and Manage a Team within Health and Social Care 84

The Features of Effective Team Performance 84

Factors that can Influence Team Performance 86

Different Challenges May Confront Developing and Established Teams 87

Overcoming Challenges 89

Effect of Different Management Styles 90

Ways to Develop Trust and Accountability 91

Different Ways to Address Conflict Within Teams 92

Components of Positive Team Culture 93

Chapter 7: Develop Professional Supervision Practice 94

Purpose of Professional Supervision in Health and Social Care 94

Theories and Models of Professional Supervision 95

Legal and Regulatory Requirements of Professional
Supervisions 97

Other Sources of Information that Need to be Filtered Down
through Supervisions: Research; Critical Reviews; Inquiries...98

The Individual, Supervisor and Supervisee: How Professional
Supervisions Can Help Protect Everyone 99

The Performance Management Cycle...................................101

The Relationship Between Performance and Professional
Supervisions 103

How Performance Indicators can be used to Measure Practice
....103

The Problem of Power Imbalance and Professional
Supervisions 104

Minimising Power Imbalances 105

Chapter 8: Ensuring positive outcomes for individuals.............106

What is Outcome-based Practice..106

Different Approaches to Outcome-Based Practice 109

Outcome-Based Practice: Impact of Legislation and Policy
Changes..111

Impact on People's Lives: the Potential Benefit of Outcome-
Based Practice 113

The Psychological Basis for Well-being 115

Systems and Processes that Promote Individual Well-Being 116

Promoting an Individual's Ability to have Choice and Control over their Decisions..117

Carers, Families and Significant Others: The Importance of Partnership Working. 118

Legislation that Promotes Partnership Working 119

Chapter 9: Safeguarding and protection of vulnerable adults ..120

Approaches to Safeguarding in your own Setting: The Impact of Policy Developments..122

Legislation Relating to Safeguarding of Vulnerable Adults ...124

Interrelationship of Serious Case Reviews and Safeguarding Processes...126

What to do: Safeguarding Protocols and Referral Procedures 128

Chapter 10: Understand safeguarding of children and young people (for those working in the adult sector) 129

Policies, procedures and practices for safe working with children and young people..129

Child Safeguarding: Legislative and Policy Guidelines...........130

Child Safeguarding: Signs, Symptoms, Indicators and Behaviours..133

In Event of Allegations of Harm or Abuse by a Child.............136

   Where Harm or Abuse is Suspected or Alleged: Rights of the Children, Young People and their Families............................137

Chapter 11: Lead and manage group living for adults 138

   Current theoretical approaches to group living provision for adults..138

   Physical group living environments: legal and regulatory requirements...142

   Maintaining the Right Balance: An Environment that is Safe and Secure, but also Promotes Freedom and Choice 145

   Link between Group Living and Positive Outcomes 149

Chapter 12: Lead person-centred practice................................150

   What is Person-centred Practice? 150

   Approaches to Person-centred Practice................................151

   Person-centred Practice: Effect of Legislation and Policy 153

   Person-centred Practice and Establishing Consent...............154

   Person-Centred Practice: Creating Positive Change in Individuals' Lives 156

Chapter 13: Assess the individual in a health and social care setting 157

   Partnership working: how this can positively influence assessment processes 160

Chapter 14: How to Respond to concerns and complaints 162

   Managing Concerns and Complaints: Regulatory Requirements and Guidance 162

   How Regulatory Requirements and Guidance Regarding Management of Concerns and Complaints affect own Service Provision 163

   Obstacles Experienced by Individuals when Raising or Making Complaints 164

   How to Encourage and Empower Individuals to use Complaints Mechanisms to Make their Voice Heard 166

Chapter 15: Facilitate change in health and social care or children and young people's setting 168

   Factors that drive change 168

   Underpinning theories of change management 171

   Supporting the Change Process: Approaches, Tools and Techniques 174

Chapter 16: Explore Models of Disability 179

   Models of Disability 179

   Different Models of Disability: How they are Experienced ... 183

   Different Models of Disability: Effect on Organisational Structures and Outcomes 184

References 188

Introduction

The health and social care sector is an ever changing landscape, and the need for skilled and intuitive managers to lead and inspire a burgeoning, highly mixed and often peripatetic workforce, has never been greater. With challenging workloads, unsociable hours and often a physical and psychological toll that is invisible from the outside, this book strives to provide a helping hand to both aspirant and current senior health and social care practitioners embarking on the Level 5 Diploma in Leadership and Management in Health and Social Care.

The book is arranged to mirror the structure of units that are required to be completed within the Diploma. I have tried to include useful learning material for each of the mandatory units, and some of the commonly chosen optional units. There is an additional book by the same author entitled, 'Understanding Autism and Positive Behavioural Support', if learners wish to undertake those units within the Diploma as well.

Understanding the theory is only part of the Level 5 Diploma. Most important of all, is being able to demonstrate in both your written and actual work practice, that you can translate your understanding into action, and describe real-life examples from your workplace, explaining and evidencing your competence and understanding.

Your assessor or tutor will guide you through your course, help structure your learning and advise you about how to evidence your competence for the performance-related assessment criteria of the course. Rather than overload the text, and make the book less accessible and concise, I have added a small guide under the heading 'Apply and Demonstrate' to help with performance-related aspects within each Unit. You will need to refer to your course booklet for the precise wording of the assessment criteria, however.

I have tried to create a book that is visually well spaced out, and not too dense, and in which the information is conveyed in an accessible, engaging way. I hope it provides you with support, and down-to-earth, useful insights.

Chapter 1: Communication

Why is Communication Important?

There are a wide variety of roles and positions that require a deeper understanding of communication in health and social care settings. Care Coordinators, Team Leaders, Unit/ Service Managers, Assistant or Deputy Managers are just some examples of the types of professional positions, where the holder of such a role would be expected not just to have excellent communication skills themselves, but to be able to anticipate the communication needs of others as well.

Such roles require a professional and comprehensive understanding of the range of groups and individuals whose communication needs must be addressed, including both professional bodies and individuals, and patient groups.

Before we examine the different communication needs of these groups and individuals, let's first pause and consider some quotations about communication, and reflect on what they tell us about the difficulties and importance of communication.

Quotations about Communication [i]

> The most important thing in communication is hearing what isn't said. (Peter Drucker)

> To effectively communicate, we must realise that we are all different in the way we perceive the world and use this understanding as a guide to our communication with others. (Tony Robbins)

> The two words 'information' and 'communication' are often used interchangeably, but they signify quite different things. Information is giving out; communication is getting through. (Sydney J. Harris)

These quotations help to remind us that communication isn't just about speaking, but also listening. Moreover, sometimes communication takes places in different ways other than verbally. This is all too apparent in health and social care settings, where service users can experience an array of conditions that affect their ability to communicate. Moreover, communication also requires the recipient to be able to process, understand and assimilate what has been communicated.

We will now look at the different groups and individuals that one will need to communicate with in a health and social care setting, and consider the needs and potential obstacles to communication:

Table 1 Groups and Individuals with Communication Needs in Health and Social Care Settings

Stakeholders in effective communication	Examples	Potential Obstacles
External organisations	- CQC (Care Quality Commission) - Local authorities - Health and Safety Executive - NHS organisations	- Separate procedures - Unclear protocols - Different management structures - Different timescales - Conflicting priorities - Resource limitations - Staff shortages
Internal professionals with a quality assurance or managerial role	- Departmental managers - Human Resources department - Operations Manager - Care Coordinators	- Financial objectives - Policies and procedures - Organisational objectives - Conflicting departmental commitments - Personality clashes
Service users		- Sensory impairment (e.g.

		visually or hearing impaired) - Memory difficulties - Communication disorder (e.g. stroke; aphasia) - Learning difficulty - Physical disability (e.g. quadriplegia; paraplegia) - English as a second language - Mental health illness (e.g. psychosis; personality disorder) - Other neurological disorder (e.g. autism; Asperger's Syndrome) - Dementia
Carers, friends and family		- Service users may struggle to maintain social networks or contact with family members, due to communication difficulties or distance, if the care setting is a long way from family/ friends. - The family may have communication support needs themselves: for

		example, Fnglish may not be their first language; they may have caring support needs themselves. - There may be conflict or tensions within families, that impacts negatively on effective communication.

How to Promote Effective communication

Effective communication is often measured subjectively. It is a difficult phenomenon to assess objectively and impartially. One way of making sure that communication has been effective, would be to ask the different parties, if they felt it was effective. You could do this by asking for oral feedback, or eliciting feedback through slightly more formal mechanisms, such as residents' meetings.

Bearing in mind the difficulty in gauging the effectiveness of communication, let us consider some of the key themes and areas that need to be assessed within an organisation to help enhance the quality of communication.

Table 2 Themes and Areas that Need to be Assessed to Help Enhance the Quality of Communication in an Organisation.

Transparency	- Are there clear lines of accountability? - Are there effective mechanisms of obtaining feedback and involvement?
Rapport with service users	- Are there comprehensive communication profiles of individual service users to ensure staff are adequately informed about how to support service users' communication needs? - Are care/ support plans detailed and sufficiently thorough?

	- Do they help to provide sufficient background for the service users? - Are regular reviews and updates about communication support needs carried out? - Are there links to other sources of professional advice: e.g. speech and language assessments; psychiatric reports/ reviews; advice from dieticians?
Skills & competencies of staff	- Some interventions that may be adopted: pictorial forms of communication; using objects of reference; using simple language; minimising background noise. - Understanding behavioural cues and signals that might indicate anxiety; depression etc. - Is any technology needed or used to support service user's communication needs? - Is there awareness or training provided about the opportunities created by assistive technology? - What training is provided at staff induction and through regular refreshers etc., to ensure effective and consistent techniques for communication are used by staff?
Communication	- How is the quality and effectiveness of

systems that are needed to ensure effective team work:	handovers ensured? - How frequently are team meetings conducted, and what sort of topics are covered? - Describe how supervisions can be utilised to ensure training needs are identified, and good practice promoted? - Do staff received regular and adequate levels of support for continuing professional development?
Risk Management	- How are risk assessments compiled, and how often are they reviewed? - Are service users involved in the identification, assessment and review of risks? - How are staff made aware of daily risk assessments, or changes to individuals care plans/ risk assessments?
Partnership working	- How do you promote partnership working with external organisations? - What is the procedure for referral to external organisations or professional services: e.g. occupational therapy; dietician support? - Do service users feel they receive a holistic and comprehensive level of support?

Barriers and Challenges to Communication

We have already touched on some of the barriers that can exist to prevent effective communication. In many ways, you can only ensure effective communication, after you have found out what those barriers or challenges are.

Moreover, often the barriers are interdependent. For example, if there is poor partnership working with speech and language services, or there is insufficient holistic support for people with visual impairment, then there isn't maybe going to be an effective rapport between staff and service users affected by speech or sight impairment.

If there is poor accountability or feedback mechanisms, then unmet communication needs will not be recognised, and will not be acted on.

On the following page, we will look at the interconnectedness and juxtaposition of these different barriers and challenges.

Table 3 Barriers and Obstacles to Effective Communication

Communication Impairments that arise directly or indirectly as a result of an underlying disability or illness.	- Dysphagia (difficulty swallowing; which can affect speech also) - Aphasia/ Dysphasia (speech impediment) - Breathing difficulties: e.g. lying down; long-term wheelchair use - Cognitive difficulties - Mental health difficulties (e.g. psychosis; hallucinations; delusions; severe depression or mania) - Brain injury - Brain tumours - Other degenerative illnesses: e.g. multiple sclerosis - Difficulty with 'executive function': e.g. being able to decide what to do next, or make plans.
Limitations to care provision	- Budgetary limitations (e.g. could hinder recruitment of skilled staff; may reduce funding available to provide training; possible reduced opportunities of quality interaction and communication between staff and service users) - Staff shortages (e.g. could lead to reliance on agency/ temporary staff, with less familiarity with communication needs of service users)

	- Transport difficulties (care provision may be difficult in more remote areas, leading to reduced interaction time between staff and service users)
Psychological barriers	- Low self-esteem - Phobias (e.g. agoraphobia) - Depression/ mood disorders - Obsessional behaviours.
Risk management	- Service users not involved in identification and management of risk - Organisations being 'risk averse' - Poor recording of risk incidents - Poor communication systems for responding to emergencies or changes in service user needs.
Departmental divisions and tensions	- Budgetary/ funding pressures on external services (e.g. physiotherapy) - Long waiting lists for referrals - Lack of take-up of expert assessments and advice by support workers and care workers.

Apply and Demonstrate

For your Level 5 Diploma, you will have to demonstrate that you can assess and respond to the different communication needs within your organisation.

Here are some aspects within your organisation that you could look at, and evaluate the strengths and weaknesses of existing communication methods, in enhancing partnership working:

- Quality of interaction and therapeutic relationships between staff and service users.
- Effectiveness of training systems and provision for continuous professional development.
- Quality assurance processes (e.g. internal and external audits and inspections)
- Processes for team management and oversight

Apply and Demonstrate

What improvements would you recommend to enhance communication systems for partnership working?

- You could write a reflective account, detailing suggested improvements, or you could produce product evidence, by way of minutes of a meeting, for example, where you put forward suggestions.
- What resources, staffing or additional expertise will be needed?
- What will be the time-frame for implementing the improvements?

Legal and Ethical Tensions Regarding Confidentiality and Sharing Information

The following laws, regulations & codes of practice all relate to this important area:

- The Caldicott Principles[ii]
- The Mental Capacity Act 2005
- Data Protection Act 1998
- Freedom of Information Act 2000

If sharing information to staff who are not part of the same team which is caring for an individual, or if the information is to be used for something other than why it was originally collected then explicit consent is required, either verbally, or in written form.

- Consent also means that the individual should have an understanding of what is being asked of them, and that they have the capacity to make the decision.
- They should be able to provide that consent voluntarily, and without any duress.
- Even if explicit consent has been obtained, it is still not allowed to share information that is unnecessary or irrelevant.
- Implied consent is involved in such instances as sharing confidential information during handovers, without the need for the patient's consent – as it is occurring within the context of the direct care of that individual.

- It is also important to note that an individual can change their consent if they wish at any time, by removing their consent. There may have been a significant change in the situation of the individual, or after a timescale that had hitherto been agreed with the organisation.

- The Data Protection Act 1998 and the Human Rights Act 1998, outline what confidential information can be shared. The Data Protection Act 1998 states that personal data can only be obtained for one or more specified and lawful purposes, and should be adequate, relevant and not excessive in relation to the purpose for which the information is being processed.

- The Human Rights Act 1998, underlines the principle of privacy, and enshrines the right of individuals to be able to live without excessive intrusion or interference into their affairs. The Act also serves to incorporate the European Convention of Human Rights into English law, which states that 'Everyone has the right to respect for his private and family life, his home and his correspondence'.

Information-sharing Protocols and Principles

Information sharing agreements need to follow the Caldicott Principles.

- The purpose for which the information is collected needs to be justified
- All personally identifiable information should be excluded unless absolutely necessary – and if so, only the minimal amount of personal identifiable information possible.
- Access to the data should be on a strict 'need to know' basis, and everyone needs to be trained, and made aware of their responsibilities towards confidentiality.
- The training needs to comply with all legal obligations: e.g. Data Protection Act 1998; Human Rights Act 1998; Police and Criminal Evidence Act 1984.
- Information should be stored securely, with clear rules and protocols in place with relation to security and access to that information.
- Information should be available in an accessible format, so that people with additional communication needs can access them.

GDPR

Data Protection has recently been amended through the introduction of the European Union General Data Protection Regulation (GDPR) in 2018. This new set of regulations tightens responsibilities for organisations, and gives regulators the power to ask for demonstrations of accountability, and also to impose fines if GDPR requirements are not adhered to.

While similar in scope and spirit to earlier Data Protection legislation, the ten key GDPR requirements are as follows:

- Lawful, fair and transparent processing: information can only be processed for a legitimate process, in a fair way, and in a transparent manner. This means that organisations should inform the owners of that data of why and how their data is being processed.
- Limitation of purpose, data and storage: organisations should only collect, process and store data when and for as long as is necessary. Once the legitimate purpose for collecting the data has been fulfilled, the personal data should be deleted.
- Data subject rights: data subjects have the right to ask what information is held about them by organisations, and what is done with their information. Data subjects can also request correction to data held about them, raise a complaint, or ask for their data to be deleted or transferred.
- Consent: Data subjects should always be consulted if their personal data is to be processed by an organisation for a reason other than the original legitimate purpose for which it

was collected. Consent must be clear, explicit and documented. Moreover, the data subject has the right to withdraw their consent at any time. Parents of children under the age of 16, must provide explicit consent for any processing of a child's data.
- Personal data breaches: it is a requirement for organisations to maintain a Personal Data Breach Register. The regulator and data subject should be notified within 72 hours of identifying the breach.
- Privacy by Design: when organisations design new systems and processes, they should incorporate organisational and technical mechanisms to protect personal data from the very first design phase.
- Data Protection Impact Assessment: when a new project, change or product is initiated, there should be a Data Protection Impact Assessment.
- Data transfers: Even if processing of personal data is being done by a third party, responsibility for ensuring the protection and privacy of that data is still part of the responsibility of the main controller of that personal data.
- Data Protection Officer: If there is a great deal of processing of personal data within an organisation, there should be appointed a Data Protection Officer, with responsibility for advising and assisting the organisation to remain compliant with EU GDPR requirements.
- Awareness and training: Organisations have a responsibility to raise and maintain awareness about key GDPR requirements amongst the workforce, and to conduct regular training.

To read further about these recent changes in legislation about data protection, please go to the following link[iii]:

http://www.wired.co.uk/article/what-is-gdpr-uk-eu-legislation-compliance-summary-fines-2018

Chapter 2: Promoting Professional Development

The Importance of Continually Improving Knowledge and Practice

Much of what drives us to improve and develop ourselves, comes from within. However, many of those ideas, opportunities and goals are also shaped by organisational factors. Often, external and internal factors operate in an interdependent way, to determine the means and direction of professional development.

When considering the importance of continuing professional development, it's important to differentiate between internal and external drivers.

Internal factors that make continuing professional development important include:

- Personal objectives
- Training needs required to be able to carry out one's role
- Expanding remit or changing responsibilities with respect to one's job description

External factors, may include:

- Demographic changes: e.g. an increasingly proportion of the population living to old age; a falling birth rate; increased rates of migration.
- Economic changes: e.g. recession; reduced levels of affordability in terms of purchasing care and support services;

housing shortages; changes to benefit systems or eligibility criteria;
- Changes to government regulations; revisions to best practice guidelines.

The following diagram also looks at these different areas:

Table 4 Why continuous professional development is important:

Changes in external environment	- Changes in technology (e.g. assistive technology; artificial intelligence) - Demographic changes (e.g. age distribution; cultural/ ethnic diversity; family structures) - Economic changes
Government regulations; regulatory requirements	- Changes to legislation and regulatory frameworks - Government White Papers (e.g. Skills for Care Workforce Development Strategy: 'Capable, Confident, Skilled' 2011[iv])
Staff skills and competency	- To ensure appropriate staff mix and competency levels within care teams - To contribute towards development of workforce as a whole - To keep up-to-date with best practice guidelines, and subject knowledge.

Potential Barriers to Professional Development

In many ways, the 'drivers' behind professional development, can also become barriers. For example, if an organisation has a requirement for a high level of training amongst its employees, then this will require a higher level of funding to fulfil such a requirement. The higher level of financial investment an organisation needs to make in training its workforce, the higher they may raise the eligibility criteria for accessing that training, in order to protect themselves from the cost of learners leaving the organisation, or finding a promotion elsewhere where they can utilise the training they have obtained.

This scenario demonstrates how internal and external barriers to professional development can sometimes be interdependent and influence one another.

What we have mentioned thus far, could be described as 'formal barriers': e.g. rules on eligibility; class sizes. One must not omit, however, the relevance of informal barriers: such as, lack of confidence, low expectations.

Often these informal barriers are disregarded, even though they have the potential to be overcome with straight-forward support, reassurance and encouragement.

The diagram below displays the different types and range of barriers to professional development:

Conscious internal factors

Negative prior experiences of learning
Lack of confidence
Lack of motivation

Unconscious internal factors

Lack of awareness or knowledge of what learning opportunities are available/ or what additional support is available for people with individual learning needs

External factors

Training provision not meeting individual learning styles sufficiently
Lack of differentiation, or support for learners with disabilities

Other external factors:

Lack of funding
Closing of some educational providers by regulators due to poor performance
Shortage of teachers

Pros and Cons of Different Methods and Approaches for Supporting Professional Development

Training Methods	Pros	Cons
Self-study (e.g. independent reading and research)	- Inexpensive - Self-driven - Helps encourage independence, learning skills and analytical skills	- Not always suitable for learners with poor motivation or low concentration. - Dependent on sufficient access to: e.g. books/ libraries/ online access.
In-house training (e.g. induction; refreshers; team meetings; supervisions & appraisals)	- Inexpensive - Internal staff can be trained to become trainers; saving expense on sourcing external trainers. - Resources can be developed in-house. - Helps promote consistency of training. - Training is focussed on the needs of the organisation, rather than being	- In-house training may not equip learners with skills and knowledge they would need in other areas of the health and social care sector. - May be limited in terms of external viewpoints or impartiality. - Staff may not feel

	'generic'.	comfortable to relay feedback if they are unhappy with the training.
External (e.g. mentoring; attending training courses).	- Encourages peer discussion and sharing of experiences. - May help provide fresh insight into work-related dilemmas. - Can be arranged in advance, with careful planning, to ensure maximum attendance.	- Can be expensive - Can be difficult to organise, as requires staff to be covered, if training takes place during work hours. - May not be relevant to work setting. - May not be supportive of individual learning needs or requirements.
Action Learning (e.g. reflective practice)	- Enables learning from real life experiences through actual work practice. - This method of learning links together organisational and individual development, through learning from real workplace issues,	- Some staff may not be motivated. - Needs follow up to ensure lessons learned are implemented. - All staff need to respect and value each other, and

| | dilemmas that occur through actual work practice and where there are no ready-made solutions. | have a commitment towards effective communication amongst one another. |

How to Weigh up and Decide on Different Approaches towards Continuous Professional Development.

When considering training for either oneself, or other staff, you need to think about the following questions:

- What training needs have been identified?
- Does it meet mandatory training requirements or standards that are expected within your role/ sector?
- Does the training opportunity fully/ or partially meet that training need?
- What level of time commitment is involved?
- Will commitment/ attendance be required?
- Will this commitment/ attendance be possible to maintain in the long term?
- Does the opportunity or activity meet career aspirations?

Think about how you have addressed these questions when deciding upon training, either for yourself or other staff in your workplace. Making the wrong choice, isn't the end of the world. We learn from mistakes. However, thinking hard about what you want the training to achieve, and how to make sure it is likely to deliver on that goal, can certainly help to minimise the risk of a waste of time and resources.

Models of Reflective Practice

Reflective Practice is an almost inseparable part of working in a health and social care setting. So diverse are the needs of patients, operational models of care providers, and so fast changing is the wider economic, technological and demographic environment, that no 'text book' could ever keep up the amount of information that needs to be relayed from one staff to the next.

Fortunately, reflective practice makes learning, and linking theory to practice, as intrinsic a part of working in a health and social care setting, as turning on the tap. There is an opportunity to learn, reflect, connect, analyse, conjecture or discuss after any patient contact, episode, or at the end of a work shift.

How we carry out reflective practice will also vary both individually, and according to how much encouragement there is in your work setting. Very often, reflective practice takes place unconsciously, such as when we reflect on the shift we have just had, on our way home from work. Other times, reflective practice takes place in more formal settings, such as during a supervision or appraisal.

For your Level 5 Diploma, you will need to be able to describe some of the different models that exist in relation to reflective practice. The figures on the following pages, outline three such models:

Kolb's Learning Cycle

Kolb sees learning and reflection as something that we do on a daily basis, through the natural experiences of life and work. He also saw learning through reflection as vital, and ongoing.

Table 5 Kolb's Learning Cycle[v]

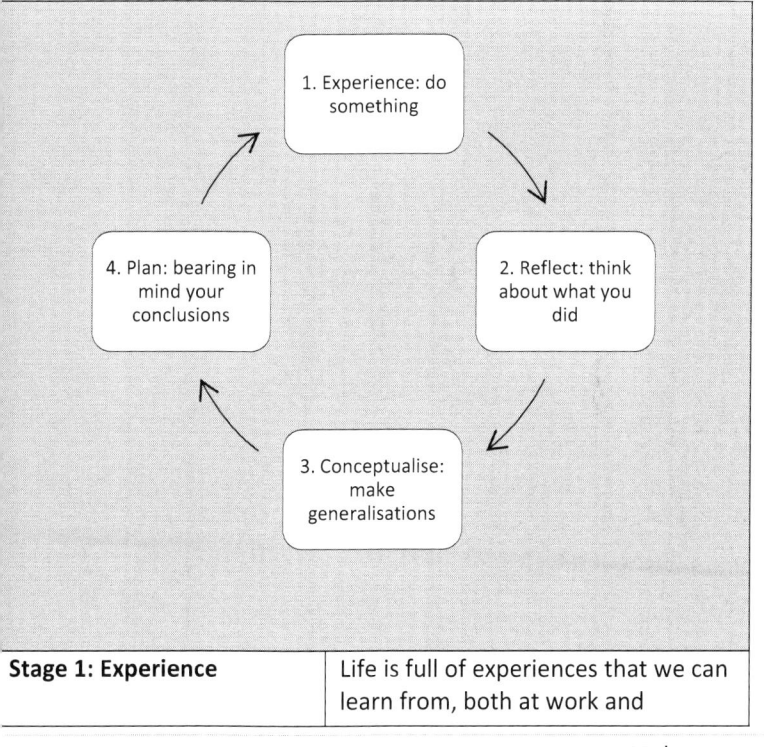

Stage 1: Experience	Life is full of experiences that we can learn from, both at work and

	beyond.
Stage 2: Reflect	This is about thinking back to your past experiences and thinking what you have learnt.
Stage 3: Conceptualise	This is about generating a hypothesis about the meaning from one's experiences.
Stage 4: Plan	This is where one tests out the hypotheses one has created, and the new experiences that arise from that will either support or challenge those hypotheses. According to Kolb, experiences only yield learning if we go through all the stages in the cycle, interpret and test our interpretations.

Gibb's Reflective Cycle

Gibbs' (1998) model[vi], represents reflection as a process with six key stages:

Description: what happened	What happened? Where & when? What did you do/ read or see? Describe other factors relevant to the context or surrounding circumstances? What were you responsible for?
Feelings: what were you thinking about?	Describe your initial reaction. Did your feelings then change at all? What were you thinking at the time?
Evaluate: What was good or bad about the experience?	What did you find difficult, upsetting or challenging during the experience? Who/ what was unhelpful? Why? What needs improvement?
Analysis: What sense can you make of the situation?	How does what you have learnt in terms of theory, compare with the situation in practice? What are the similarities or differences between this situation and other experiences?
Conclusion	What have you learnt for the future? What else could you have done?
Action Plan: What will you do next time?	If a similar situation arose again, what would you do?

Johns' Model for Structured Reflection

Johns' (2000) model[vii], is applicable to a broad range of fields, although it was originally developed for nursing practitioners. His model is structured based on two concepts, 'Looking in' and 'Looking out', as displayed below:

Looking in:

- Find a space to focus on oneself
- Pay attention to your thoughts and emotions
- Write down these thoughts and emotions

Looking out:

- Write a description of the situation
- What issues seem significant?
- What was I trying to achieve? Why did I respond as I did? What were the consequences for me and others? How were others feeling? How did I know this?
- Personal feelings: Why did I feel the way I did within this situation?
- Ethics: Did I act for the best?
- What factors were influencing me?
- What knowledge did or could have informed me?
- Reflexivity: How does this situation relate to previous experiences? How could I have handled this better? What would have been the consequences of alternative actions? How do I feel now about the experience? How can I support myself and others better in the future?

Explain the importance of reflective practice to improve performance

Reflective practice helps you to process, digest and assimilate information, that has been gained through work experience. These terms are described in the table below.

Aspects to reflective practice:	What does this mean in practice?	Why this is important:
Process	- Discussing with peers something that has happened at work; - Thinking about it; describing what happened in a report; - Rationalising something; - Making sense of it.	- Helps us to sort out one's emotions - Helps us to stay in tune with new experiences and not 'switch off'
Digest	- Coming up with theories or hypotheses as to why something happened; developing more understanding about it; getting feedback from others about one's thoughts about an experience	- Helps us gain a deeper understanding of new ideas - Prevents ideas getting lost or forgotten

Assimilate	- Incorporating the ideas you have learnt into your everyday work practice; changing one's approaches at work or how one does things; sharing one's learning with peers	- Harnesses new ideas, and makes one's work style and practices intuitively connected to one's surroundings - Enables one to become a more empathetic, responsive, person-centred provider of care and support.

Apply and Demonstrate

For your Level 5 Diploma, you will need to show that you can and do engage with reflective practice, and that you actively use this to drive your professional development.

You could achieve this by writing a reflective essay, talking about an episode or situation that you found difficult, using the stages highlighted in the reflective practice models described earlier. [502: 4.3-4.4]

Chapter 3: Championing Equality, Diversity and Inclusion

Models of Practice that Underpin Equality, Diversity and Inclusion

Diversity
About valuing difference & demonstrating that value
Supporting service users to have an active voice and to be able to participate in all areas of their care.
That all views and perspectives are valued and respected equally

Equality
People are NOT the same.
However, each and every one of us, should be treated equally, without differentiation according to disability, religion, gender, race, age, sexual orientation etc.

Inclusion
The principle of inclusion, reflects the reality that because of diversity, some individuals need more support to enjoy parity or a sense of equality than others
Proactive measures are needed to ensure equal treatment and opportunity.
The principles of diversity, equality and inclusion, are important both in terms of service provision and management and workforce development.

Potential Effects of Barriers to Equality and Inclusion

Types of barriers	How these barriers can have an effect:	Example:
Physical barriers – e.g. mobility impairments	May limit independence, and have a negative effect on physical health	e.g. makes maintenance of mobility aids extremely important
Attitudinal barriers	May limit opportunities to support physical or mental health improvement. People may encounter stigma when they attempt to find work or make connections with the social community.	e.g. may make individuals with mental health problems scared to engage with the community, or develop social networks
Institutional barriers	Individuals may feel discriminated against or disadvantaged as a result of certain policies and procedures	e.g. individuals may feel like they can't open up and confide in those who are employed to look after them

Oppression	If barriers are not addressed, or prevail and get worse, they can develop into a cycle of oppression. Active discrimination and prejudice become the 'norm' or 'systematised'. The target groups often internalise or 'buy into' aspects of oppression, and then conform to the perceived stereotypes.	e.g. sufferers of abuse, not reporting their abusers.

The Impact of Legislation and Policy Initiatives

Legislation:	Summary:	Example of impact:
Equality Act 2010[viii]	Improved consistency in the law, and incorporates previous legislation (e.g. Race Relations Act 1976 & Disability Discrimination Act 1995) into one piece of legislation. Set up the Commission for Equality and Human Rights The Act made it a duty on the part of all public authorities to promote equality of opportunity for men and women, and to prevent sex discrimination. Incorporated 'age discrimination' into the Act. The Act also extended protections to people who identify as transgender, and individuals who are associated with another person who has a disability,	Improved care provision for elderly people, especially with dementia care, in residential and nursing homes.

	e.g. a carer.	
Disability Discrimination Act 2005	A mainstay in the history of legislation for the promotion of rights of disabled people. Outlined a requirement of public organisations to ensure there are accessible facilities for disabled people (e.g. access; toilets; interpretation)	The Act helped to remove some of the barriers and discrimination experienced by disabled people, in such areas as: employment; education; access to goods; facilities and services; buying or renting land or property; and the function of public bodies. The Act has been now replaced by the 2010 Equality Act, although the Disability Equality Duty is still in use.
Equal Pay Act	Stipulates that employers	Has helped

1970	cannot discriminate between men and women by paying them differently or providing different employment terms and conditions, if they are doing the same or similar work, work of equal value, or work that is rated as equivalent in a job evaluation scheme.	improve work performance and work relations, by removing an area of inequality.
Sex Discrimination Act 1975 (and amendments 1982 & 1999)	Made it illegal to discriminate against someone on the basis of sex, marital status or gender reassignment. This applies to recruitment procedures, setting terms and conditions, promotion and training opportunities and termination of employment.	Has improved working relations, which has a beneficial impact on services received by the public.
Race Relations Act 1976 (amendments 2000 & 2003)	Placed a duty on public authorities to promote race equality on a statutory footing	

How to Promote Equality, Diversity and Inclusion

As the saying goes, 'action speaks louder than words': and this is certainly true when it comes to the issue of promoting equality. Whether 'it feels' as if equality, diversion and inclusion is promoted within an organisation, will often depend on who you ask: the staff, the management, the patients, the family/friends of service users. Therefore, promoting of these values and concepts in many ways goes in tandem with the development of effective and inclusive communication within an organisation.

In addition to this, it is also important to remember that it is important to look at mechanisms for promoting equality and inclusion amongst the workforce, as well as amongst the client-group. This is important, and sometimes overlooked. If there are staff who feel subjected to racism, sexism or ageism, then this can affect their morale or ways of working, which can be easily noticed, and give rise to concern or anxiety amongst service users as well.

On the next page, are some suggestions for promoting equality and inclusivity in a social care setting. They are no means exhaustive, and indeed what works for different teams and different settings, in different contexts, is up to the skill and insight of a manager to assess, and respond to.

Table 6 Ways to Promote Equality, Diversity and Inclusion

- Ensuring service users have a voice and are heard
- Managing staff allocation, so that service users are supported by support workers with relevant skills and competencies.
- Focussing on service user outcomes, to ensure that the support provided is actually making a difference where it matters, with relevant skillset.
- Managing the different support and learning needs of the workforce (e.g. staff with learning/ or physical disabilities).
- Encouraging respect and tolerance for different view, with regular opportunities for discussion: e.g. team meetings.
- Ensuring there is a positive and open climate for communication.

Apply and Demonstrate

How do you challenge discrimination and exclusion from within your role? How could you evidence this?

You might be able to show how you have raised an issue during a team meeting, and have seen it through by implementing extra training, or carrying out additional observations and relaying feedback to staff? Maybe you have generated feedback from service users during residents' meetings, or during monthly reviews?

Whatever example you are able to demonstrate and describe, you need to be able to show that you didn't just 'notice' an instance of discrimination and exclusion: but that you acted on it.

Interventions can Both Promote Equality and Inclusion: or Reinforce Discrimination and Exclusion

Promoting equality and inclusion is an ongoing process, and not one that can be accomplished overnight. There are workforce changes, variations in composition and health of service users or patient groups, and at times there will be changes to management structures. There can be both internal and external drivers of change, that can destabilise the most harmonious of teams.

Deciding what to do and when to do it, from the role of manager, is a matter of judgement and careful management. Especially so, as sometimes interventions that are carried out with the best of intentions, have unexpected consequences and don't produce the desired effects.

Sometimes different groupings within a workforce can experience different needs or pressures when it comes to inclusion. For example, an organisation may operate with a diverse workforce, some of whom may not speak English as their first language, or identify with BME (black and ethnic minority) communities. At the same time, there may be other forms of identity by staff within a workforce: as a result, some employees may experience discrimination on the basis of feminism or ageism. The role of the manager is not to respond to staff clashes on the basis of 'prima facie' evidence of discrimination. Often, there can different perceptions of discrimination and pressures of inclusion.

A manager has to seek to create a channel that enables everyone to have a voice, for no 'one' individual or grouping to have an advantage over another, and where everyone is treated, and learns to treat each other, with equanimity and respect. Responses that are overly one-sided, hasty or judgemental may be more likely to invoke even greater feelings of discrimination, and exacerbate workforce tensions even further.

Effectiveness of Systems and Processes in Promoting Equality, Diversity and Inclusion

Apply and Demonstrate

You need to think introspectively, and analytically, here to assess where and how your current organisation is 'working well' and 'working less well' with regards to promoting equality, diversity and inclusion.

For example, it may be that you feel that there are good communication systems and feedback mechanisms with service users, carers, friends and family. However, it may also be that there have been instances of negative feedback, which have prompted you to recommend certain changes and improvements.

It may be that there is a lot of effort in ensuring provision of training in equality and diversity, and yet there have still emerged

	Apply and Demonstrate
	Based on your analysis of issues earlier, what would you suggest would be needed areas of improvement in your organisation?
	How urgent are those improvements?
	What would happen if those improvements were not made?
	What will be the impact of the improvements?
	Who do you need to involve to help implement the improvements?
	Are there any other resources or expertise you need to source, to help you implement the changes?

Ethical Dilemmas: Balancing Rights and Duty of Care

Recognising, and developing ways to respond to ethical dilemmas, is a crucial dimension of working within the health and social care sector.

Ethical dilemmas can arise for lots of different reasons. In the diagram below, are some examples, although you should be able to identify, analyse and describe similar dilemmas that arise within your work practice.

Where a service user is experiencing abuse, but asks for this not to be disclosed to anyone ...
Where a service user chooses to do something that is unsafe or potentially harmful, and staff need to balance their right to make their own choices, and also fulfil their duty of care...
Where a service user with a learning disability talks about wanting a boyfriend or girlfriend...
A service user is getting bored and frustrated after staying indoors all day, and has been throwing things and shouting. Should they still be supported to go out, or have what they had been looking forward to taken away?

The Concept of Informed Choice

- Where an individual needs support to: obtain relevant information; process & understand it; weigh it up.
- Where the individual takes on board a shared responsibility for the choices they make and the outcomes
- Information is presented in an accessible way according to their needs

- Information is unbiased and presented in an evidence-based format

- Family members, advocates or other professionals, have been consulted as appropriate.

- The environment or care setting is an enabling and empowering one, and no duress has been placed on the individual making the decision

How Issues affecting Mental Capacity can Influence Informed Choice

- Under the Mental Capacity Act 2005, it is important to assume that everyone has the capacity to make their own decisions
- Individuals who have cognitive impairment, may be assessed as being unable to make some decisions, but not all. An assessment of an individual's ability to make a decision, should be assessed for each individual decision.
- As much support should be given as necessary to help individuals to reach decisions, and to access sufficient and relevant information.
- Individuals have the right to make 'unwise' decisions.
- Capacity may be impaired by physical or mental health issues (e.g. coma; unconsciousness)

To research further about this topic, go to the following links:
https://www.nhs.uk/conditions/consent-to-treatment/[ix]

https://www.scie.org.uk/mca/introduction/using-mental-capacity-act[x]

Apply and Demonstrate

- What areas have you identified as needing improvement in relation to the concept of positive risk management in your organisation?
- How do you propose to improve the facilitation of informed choices, enablement and helping people to manage risks?
- How can you enhance active participation?

To explore further the concept of positive risk management, go to the following link:

https://www.scie.org.uk/publications/ataglance/ataglance31.asp

Chapter 4: Promoting Health and Safety

The Legislative Framework for Health, Safety and Risk Management

Legislation:	Summary:
The Health and Safety Act 1974 & Management of Health and Safety at Work Regulations (1999)	The 1974 Act enshrines the responsibility of employers towards employees and the public in general, to ensure that adequate training, working environments and equipment are provided. An employer or employee must take steps to ensure the health and safety and wellbeing of employees and others are protected 'so far as is reasonably practical'. The 1999 Regulations stipulate the responsibility of managers to undertake risk assessments to ensure the safety of their workplaces, and communicate these risk assessments to the employees and relevant personnel.
Workplace (Health and	Identifies the broader range of aspects

Safety and Welfare) Regulations 1992	of a workplace that are the responsibility of an employer to ensure are safe: e.g. issues like ventilation; heating; lighting; workstations; seating and welfare facilities.
Personal Protective Equipment at Work Regulations (1992)	States that employers have to make sure that appropriate protective clothing and equipment are available for employees.
Provision and Use of Work Equipment Regulations Act 1998	Outlines the responsibility of employers to ensure the safe provision of appropriate equipment in the workplace, and also to ensure that there are effective procedures in place for maintenance, repair, and training in its use.
Health and Safety Information for Employees Regulations 1989	States that employers have to have a poster that tells employees the basic information that they need to know about health and safety.
Employers' Liability (Compulsory Insurance) Act 1969	States that it is compulsory for all employers to have up-to-date and relevant insurance to cover them for accidents and ill health to their employees.
Reporting of Injuries, Diseases and Dangerous	The Act makes it explicit that employers have to notify the relevant authorities

Occurrences Regulations (1995) (RIDDOR)	about certain occupational injuries, diseases and dangerous event within 7 days.
The Electricity at Work Regulations Act 1989	States that employers or employees in control of electrical systems must ensure that they are safe to use, and that they have been maintained in a safe condition.
The Control of Substances Hazardous to Health Regulations 2002 (COSHH)	Outlines the responsibility of employees to have risk assessments in place to ensure control of any hazardous substances, and have appropriate precautions in place.
Health and Safety (First Aid) Regulations 1981	Describes the requirements of employers to have adequate first aid handlers, training and equipment on site.
Food Safety Act 1990	Outlines the statutory obligation to treat food that is intended for human consumption, in a controlled and manged way. Food must comply with food safety requirements, and be 'of the nature, substance and quality demanded', and be correctly described and labelled.
Regulatory Reform (Fire	States that it is the responsibility of an

| Safety) Order 2005 | employer or organisation to identify, manage and reduce the risk of fire. |

Apply and Demonstrate

Much of this unit, within the Level 5 Diploma, is about *performance* and demonstrating workplace competence.

Your tutor or assessor will guide you through the performance-related assessment criteria for this unit. In broad summary, however, this is what you will have to show/ and some examples of how you could show it:

In relation to health, safety and risk management policies and procedures:

- Individual compliance (e.g. risk assessments carried out and reviewed; health and safety audits)
- Support provided for other members of the workforce to ensure compliance
- Show ability to explain procedures and protocol if staff do not fully understand or comply with their health and safety responsibilities (e.g. Additional training; spot-checks; coaching & mentoring; work shadowing; disciplinary procedures)
- Compliance with record-keeping and report requirements.
- Show own work competency with regards to identifying, assessing and managing risk assessments

Maintaining and Helping Others to Sustain a Balanced Approach to Risk Management

> Read the following resource before addressing these questions:
> https://www.scie.org.uk/publications/ataglance/ataglance31.asp

Consider the following questions[xi]:

- What are you doing well at the moment?
- What areas could you improve upon?
    - For example:
    - Ensuring better prompt/ accurate reporting of accidents & injuries;
    - Improving attitudes towards risk management;
    - Promoting a better balance regarding risk aversion and promoting individual rights;
    - Dealing with conflict of opinion;
    - Providing effective mediation when dealing with conflicts and dilemmas?

It is also important to be able to help others in the workforce understand how to balance rights and risk management. Otherwise, there is a risk of a 'two-tier' structure within the workforce developing:

one that is less risk averse than the other. This can cause a lot of frustration, confusion, and lack of consistency for service users. Moreover, in an overly risk-averse setting, this can sometimes lead to service users or clients feeling the need to take risks in a covert way, but without any support at all, which increases the risk of more serious harm or injury.

Sometimes there can be a misunderstanding of boundaries. Staff may misinterpret the issue of 'balance', and allow service users to 'do what they want to do', and not be intuitive enough or ensure they are available to anticipate potential accidents or respond to things if they go wrong.

On the other hand, sometimes stereotypes based on what certain types of people are perceived to be able to do, or not to do, can influence the level of encouragement provided by carers. For example, sometimes it is thought that people with certain disabilities just 'shouldn't do' certain things. These thoughts may be based more on prejudice than on a true representation of a person's needs or support requirements.

Here are some ways in which you can help increase understanding about promoting a balance between risk management and rights:

- Develop an open work climate, where staff feel able to question 'status quo', talk about incidents, anxieties at work, dilemmas.
- Develop mechanisms where service users can also have an input in decisions made, and be involved in discussions about risk management (e.g. during reviews; residential meetings)

Apply and Demonstrate

Obtain feedback about existing policies and procedures about health and safety: are there areas that staff or clients would like to see improvement in?

Evaluate existing health and safety provision:
- What's working and what is working less well?
- Are there any areas of health & safety that could be improved to ensure better compliance with legislation and regulations?
- How do you currently audit your compliance in relation to health and safety?
- What do you feel are the strengths with regards to health and safety in your organisation?
- Where are the weaknesses?

Identify areas that need improvement:
- How urgent are the improvements that you have identified?
- What will happen if they aren't improved?
- What impact would the improvements have?

Recommend changes:
- Who will you need to involve in the proposed changes?
- Are there any additional resources, or budgetary requirements, that you will need to implement the changes?

Chapter 5: Work in Partnership in Health and Social Care

Features of Partnership Working

Since the 1999 Health Act, there has been an increasing focus within health and social care, to promote smarter and more joined-up working between health and social care services. There has been a growing understanding that it is important for individuals to be able to have access, and choice, from a range of services, to help ensure they receive more person-centred treatment early on, to prevent problems becoming more acute and harder to treat.

Key features of partnership working must therefore include:
- Promoting choice and control
- Person-centred services that involves individuals, their families and carers
- Preventative and holistic services
- Services should seek to promote mental well-being as well as physical health.

This list is by no means exhaustive. Can you think of other features that are important to partnership working? How do you translate those ideas into practice in your own work setting?

There is no concrete 'hard-and-fast' definition of what partnership working means. On the next page, are some different varying interpretations of the term:

Table 7 Different Interpretations of Partnership-Working

Cooperation	- Communicating effectively, in timely-fashion, and consistently. - Carrying out report-writing; audit and other quality-control processes effectively and reliably.
Conflict management	- Effective use of regular professional supervision meetings - Effective leadership style, which makes staff feel valued, and having a sense of ownership and 'buy-in' into the organisation's mission. - Prompt and effective responding to concerns, complaints and grievances.
Collaboration	- Working as a team or in partnership with others to help produce or achieve something: e.g. a shared goal; research project; Key Performance Indicators (e.g. customer feedback; CQC ratings).
Shared Learning:	- Having a commitment to learning and development to help ensure the organisation as a whole, experiences continuous improvement. - Display effective collaboration with external sources of expertise or professionals, and integrating advice or recommendations into

	one's own work practice.
Community Empowerment	- On a different level, when working in social care, one should think not just of those who work in the same organisation or profession as you, but those who work in the NHS, or public health. - Since the 2010 White Paper 'Equity and Excellence: Liberating the NHS', and the Health and Social Care Bill in 2011, there has been an emphasis on community empowerment through collaborative services across the NHS, public health and social services. - This has been exemplified by the setting up of Health and Well-Being Boards, which are in charge of commissioning local integrated services.

Partnership Working: with Colleagues; Other Professionals; Others

The value of partnership working is clearly apparent. However, in practice, partnership working can be harder to achieve in reality, because different groups and individuals want or expect different kinds or forms of partnership working.

In the following table, we will examine why partnership working is important to different groups of people, how this can contribute to better outcomes, and possible ways to overcome potential obstacles.

The variety of settings in health and social care is huge. Therefore, when writing about this issue towards the Level 5 Diploma, it is important to contextualise your analysis, and describe approaches that are used in your own setting.

	Why partnership working is important and can contribute to better outcomes	Ways to overcome potential obstacles
Colleagues	- Working effectively together can help meet targets and recommendations set	- Cascade down targets and recommendations to ensure all team

	by external regulators, e.g. CQC: and contribute to safer and more effective care and support delivered to service users. - Effective communication will enhance consistency of working, and help promote wellbeing amongst service users.	members are aware and focussed on achieving shared goals. - Identify, and propose improvements to prevent inconsistencies or errors in communication: e.g. guidance about how to deliver effective handovers; training to reduce instances of mistakes in record-keeping.
Other Professionals	- Working collaboratively with external professionals, such as Speech and Language Therapists or Occupational Therapists, can help provide better holistic care to individuals	- Make sure recommendations from external professionals are relayed to all levels of staffing, and that they are implemented: e.g. support for service users

	and promote better individual outcomes.	affected by dysphagia (difficulty swallowing); or daily exercises recommended by physiotherapists.
Others	- Working supportively with family members and carers, can help create a channel of communication between the individual being cared for, and others that they themselves depend on. This can help to improve knowledge and understanding of an individual's needs, and support their family and carers with the psychological support needs to maintain contact and role in the individual's wellbeing.	- Focus on building trust and creating empathetic working relationships, to put carers and families at their ease and to feel able to open up about perceived barriers or obstacles.

Apply and Demonstrate

Show that you can explain and demonstrate what your role and responsibilities are in terms of working *with colleagues, other professionals and others [e.g. family/ carers]*:
- Show how you develop procedures for effective working relationships.
- Show how you develop and agree common objectives
- Show you can evaluate the working relationships
- And deal with conflict constructively

Chapter 6: Lead and Manage a Team within Health and Social Care

The Features of Effective Team Performance

Team's evolve and develop much the same as other types of relationships do: sometimes for the better, and sometimes for the worse!

There have been a number of theories put forward, which seek to encapsulate the key stages that teams go through when they develop, in order to help managers be able to identify when and how problems can arise.

According to Bruce Tuckman's phases of team development[xii]:

- The initial phase is characterised by the phrase, 'team forming' or just 'Forming'. This is the stage where roles and responsibilities within a team are still being clarified.
- He described the second stage as 'Storming', which is where this is competition within the group, when individuals compete for position or power, and ideas get challenged.
- The development of a consensus, or 'Norming', gradually takes place as ground rules become set, and roles and responsibilities become clearly defined and accepted.
- Only at the final, 'Performing' stage, is effectiveness at its height, although disagreements may still occur.

Tuckman believed that team performance is something that develops over time, but is chiefly characterised by internal conflict, and countervailing efforts to respond to them.

> Watch the following YouTube clip here to learn a little more about Tuckman's theory of team development:
> https://www.youtube.com/watch?v=nFE8IaoInQU

Another model put forward by Syer and Connolly (1996), sees teams as more determined by *inputs*, such as the size or structure of the team, and how this is transformed into *outputs* as a result of *structural processes*, such as planning, problem solving and decision making.

This model suggests that effectiveness can be maximised at any stage of a team's development if there are robust enough systems and processes within it to hold it together.

Factors that can Influence Team Performance

While by no means exhaustive, here are some examples of factors that can have an either negative or positive effect of tea performance. Have these factors, or any others, influenced team performance within your organisation?

- The right skill-mix within a team
- Adequate training
- Communication systems
- Cooperative working and consistency
- Even distribution of work/ tasks
- Leadership
- Accountability
- Effective oversight; reduction of occurrences of 'bad practice'; standard setting
- Morale
- Sense of mission

Different Challenges May Confront Developing and Established Teams

A developing team might be characterised by a group of employees who have no previous experience of working for each other, or who have been appointed by a newly or recently formed organisation.

An established team is where a group of employees have worked for each other for a long time, and don't have such difficulties as lack of familiarity with other colleagues, or processes, to contend with as much. Nevertheless, the challenges facing an established team, can be no less serious. In fact, fatigue, and entrenched 'bad practice' are potentially a greater hazard, the more 'established' a team becomes.

The table below, looks at the potential contrasts between the challenges felt by these two different types of teams:

Table 8 Challenges Facing Developing and Established Teams

Developing teams…	Established teams…
- Inadequate training - Lack of trust - Poor skill mix - Poor communication systems - Not understanding roles and responsibilities - Lack of leadership - Poor accountability - Poor morale - Bad practice not dealt with - Poor focus - Lack of familiarity with each other - Unfamiliar with setting - Internal rivalry - Lack of familiarity with care plans	- Bad practice may have become accustomed to - May experience 'drift'; lack of focus - Team members working independently and not 'as a team' - Not willing to try out new ideas - Lack of creativity - Unwillingness to listen to criticism or new ideas. - 'False consensus': people show agreement to things, but actually do not.

Overcoming Challenges

Here is a scattering of ideas that can help overcome the obstacles to team performance. Can you think of other ideas or approaches you currently utilise?

- Promote a climate of openness
- Encourage feedback and learning
- See mistakes as a learning opportunity
- Resolve conflicts swiftly
- Maintain a no tolerance approach to bullying
- Conduct regular team meetings
- Undertake regular observations/ staff supervisions: make sure instructions and training are being listened to
- Give positive feedback

Effect of Different Management Styles

Three main styles of leadership: autocratic; paternalistic and democratic[xiii].

- Autocratic: the manager takes decisions themselves with no advice from others
- Paternalistic: the manager listens to others, and bases decisions on what is best for the company and the staff, but still makes decisions themselves and unilaterally
- Democratic: Decisions are made in the group, and voted on.

Different styles of leadership are appropriate for different situations:
- For example, in a crisis situation: would a democratic, autocratic or paternalistic be more appropriate?
- Which form of leadership would be more appropriate for newly formed teams as opposed to well-established teams?

When is it a good thing to delegate decision making?

There is a difference between 'management' and 'leadership'... Most leaders are managers of some kind, but not all managers are leaders!

Ways to Develop Trust and Accountability

Trust is developed and generated through character and competence. In other words, trust in one's professional competence is developed by how one behaves towards others, and the effectiveness of one's decisions.

- **Character** is not just about behaviour, but also intentions and motives. It is important that one's decisions are fair and balanced, and are focussed on the values that are intrinsic to the care organisation, such as a commitment to compassion, and working in a person-centred way.

- **Competence**: is about having the right skills to do the job; being up-to-date with one's knowledge and training; with an ability to work with a sense of confidence, safety and reliability.

Other ingredients of 'trust', must surely include:
- Integrity;
- Accountability;
- A willingness to learn from mistakes
- Communication skills: being able to promote an open climate of communication; demonstrating active listening skills
- Responding to problems or crises in a collaborative/ democratic way
- Carrying out the following effectively and in a time-manner: Record keeping; quality assurance processes; procedures relating to monitoring and review; effective compliance with regulations.

Different Ways to Address Conflict Within Teams

Fisher and Ury (1983) have described a concept called *'principled negotiation'* for dealing with conflicts, and it is based on four principles[xiv]:

- Separate the people from the problem: focus on service needs rather than personality or individual issues.
- Focus on interests not positions: (don't let your judgement get clouded by someone's position or power)
- Try to generate a variety of options before trying to reach mutual agreement (don't just try to impose one solution)
- Make sure that agreement is based only on objective criteria, and that it is fair, reasonable and agreeable.

'Team Roles[xv]': Another method of addressing conflict is through the concept of 'team roles', developed by Belbin. He sees teams as composed of individuals with different behavioural strengths and weaknesses, which can be summed up in terms of nine roles.

Belbin argues that seeing each team member as unique, encourages teams members to value one another, and to make allowances for weaknesses.

Some team members may show characteristics of more than one role. Managers should try to have a balance of different characteristics or traits within a team though. If there are too many 'shapers' then this could cause internal conflict and in-fighting.

The concept of team roles, encourages team members to be self-reflective, and to be proud of their strengths and feel encouraged to use them, but also to be conscious of their weaknesses too, and to try to minimise them.

1. Plants: could be unorthodox or forgetful
2. Resource investigators: might forget to follow up on a lead
3. Monitor evaluators: could be overly critical and slow moving
4. Co-ordinators: might over delegate leaving themselves little work to do
5. Implementers: might be slow to relinquish their plans in favour of positive changes
6. Completer finishers: could be accused of taking their perfectionism to the extremes
7. Team workers: might become indecisive when unpopular decisions need to be made
8. Shapers: could risk becoming aggressive and bad-humoured in their attempts to get things done
9. Specialist: may have a tendency to focus narrowly on their own subject of choice

The nine roles that Belbin outlines are as follows:

Components of Positive Team Culture

Positivity: ability to think creatively; interest in career development; tackle challenges and to work cooperatively.

Martin Seligman[xvi], described a model called the 'PERMA Model', which outlines the following attributes of a positive leader: positive emotion;

engagement; positive relationships; meaning; accomplishment/ achievement.

Chapter 7: Develop Professional Supervision Practice

Purpose of Professional Supervision in Health and Social Care

Supervisions are often underestimated. Carried out well, supervisions have the potential to help harness positive energies within a team, sharpen focus, forge trust between management and workforce, drive change and build motivation.

As a starter, let's have a look at some of the reasons why supervisions are carried out. The reasons are very wide-ranging, and it will soon become apparent, that there is a skill – perhaps even an art – to getting them right!

Purpose of Supervisions	To make sure staff are held accountable for good and poor practice
	So that managers can determine the training needs of their staff
	To help build good relationships between employer and supervisees
	To help staff identify areas of development, and become involved in their professional development.
	To encourage staff to come to you with any difficulties or grievances they might have.

| | To help sort out problems before they escalate |

Theories and Models of Professional Supervision

A number of theorists have proposed different models to help us look at the different functions, and ways of carrying out supervisions. A process that is often dismissed as an 'unnecessary bureaucratic chore', the following models bring into relief the importance of supervisions, and carrying them out properly.

Cutliffe and Proctor 1998: The 'Functional Model of Supervision'.	They argued supervisions should be: - Restorative/ supportive: to help the member of staff address stress or destress caused by problems at work. - Normative/ managerial: with the focus on monitoring and evaluation of an employees' work, with focus on looking at how to enhance quality of work performance and adherence to professional standards. - Formative/ educative: where there is a focus on identifying training and development needs and skills
Myers 2008:	He outlined a more solution-focussed approach, which was about empowering others by helping them think about positive ways to deal with problems.

Davys and Beddoe 2010:	They outlined a more detailed functional model of supervision. In their view, supervision was about three key elements: - Management: implementing policies, procedures, monitoring quality of work, making decision and priorities - Reflective: focussing on the practitioner's work - Facilitating development: CPD, evaluating knowledge and skills against benchmarks and codes of practice. - All these aspects work better when there is a strong relationship between supervisor and supervisee.

Legal and Regulatory Requirements of Professional Supervisions

Can organisations get away with providing no supervisions at all? Are they 'really' that important? The answer to both those questions, are 'no' and 'yes', and there is legal underpinning as well to the requirement of supervisions, as well as training, to be facilitated and delivered effectively.

Employers have to provide training and supervision, because this is outlined in legislation, in particular the Health and Social Care Act Regulations which set up the Care Quality Commission in 2009.

Health and social care workers also have to follow the Code of Practice written by Skills for Care, and Point 6 of this relates to continuous professional development.

Employers have to provide information about training to the National Minimum Data Set for Social Care (NMDS-SC), run by Skills for Care, which helps to monitor the training needs of the sector as a whole.

Some organisations require supervisions every month, but some only every 3 months. Every organisation will have different requirements.

Other Sources of Information that Need to be Filtered Down through Supervisions: Research; Critical Reviews; Inquiries.

Research:	The National Institute for Health and Clinical Excellence was established in 1999, to help produce and make available evidence-based research as well. You could go to the NICE website, to find up-to-date guidance for how to support someone with a particular condition.
Serious case reviews:	Serious case reviews: help us to learn lessons from serious incidents where there has been a massive service failure and a service user has died or experienced neglect. For example, the scandal at Winterbourne View, lead to a government paper called, 'Transforming Care', which set out an aim to end the practice of individuals with earning difficulties or autism remaining too long in in appropriate settings, like hospitals or residential settings.
	They are all ways of getting evidence-based research, and making sure that lessons learnt are disseminated to the team as a whole.

The Individual, Supervisor and Supervisee: How Professional Supervisions Can Help Protect Everyone

> The following video shows the importance of supervision within the health and social care sector, by the Social Care Institute for Excellence:
> https://www.youtube.com/watch?v=ERymMtmq9MQ

Supervisions Help to Protect:	
The Individual/ Service User/ Patient:	They help to make sure staff have the right knowledge and skills for the job, to iron out bad practice, and pick up on problems early. They also help to provide a private space where they can share concerns, which in turn helps with morale and well-being. Staff with a positive sense of morale and well-being, are more likely to be able to carry out their role effectively, and report concerns to management in good time.
The Supervisor	Supervisions help managers to identify training needs as a whole, and so also help therefore with workforce development planning as a whole. As well as this, they also help ensure training is

	delivered consistently and effectively, to help prevent mistakes happening. They promote accountability, as actions set are recorded, and easily monitored and reviewed. They also help enable private concerns from family, other staff or service users to able to be passed on confidentially.
The Supervisee	Supervisions can be very positive opportunities, that enable supervisees/ staff members to share problems they might be having, or to ask for guidance or training about the job. Alternatively, some employees may be experiencing personal problems, such as family difficulties/ childcare; bereavement; or bullying/ harassment in the workplace.
	Without regular supervisions, these problems can become 'buried' or 'bottled up', until they culminate in either the staff member having to go off sick, or leaving employment altogether.
	More generally, supervisions help staff members to ensure they get regular feedback and training, which can in turn help to build a sense of ownership and morale, and keep stress at bay.

The Performance Management Cycle

A structure to the supervisory process, that is incorporated with the Performance Management Cycle[xvii], is important for a number of reasons. As we shall see, there are certain stages to the performance management cycle, and it does not help to get these in the wrong order!

Perhaps you have experience yourself, on receiving negative feedback for an aspect of performance, that you didn't know was going to be measured or was a target? Or perhaps you have experienced management processes that didn't feel transparent, and that decisions were arrived at without due process being followed?

The I&DeA 2007[xviii]:

Outlined four main stages to the performance management cycle:

- Firstly, the performance management cycle begins with the planning stage, in terms of annually made agreements for forthcoming targets and objectives;
- Secondly, the manager must do supervisions during the year;
- He/she then does the review by way of the formal appraisal process;
- And then they finally revise and adjust any standards as necessary.

This model is seen as a good structure, as it is transparent and simple to follow, and is the model most tend to expect in workplaces, and want to see as a minimum in terms of support.

Armstrong's model, 2009:

- First stage: objectives are agreed;
- Secondly: the method for measuring outputs will be defined and agreed upon;
- Thirdly: feedback is given on performance and positive encouragement to reinforce good practice is given;
- And lastly: dialogue about ideas or suggestions for areas to develop takes place.

This model emphasises the importance of feedback and dialogue, and the importance of having a shared understanding of the needs of the organisation.

There are also three main theories that underline the performance management cycle:

- Control theory: has an emphasis on the importance of feedback for managing good behaviour and correcting bad practice/ performance.
- Goal theory: focusses on agreed objectives that the organisation is striving for.
- Social cognitive theory: focusses on developing amongst employees a positive sense of self-belief, as this can also have an impact on performance.

The Relationship Between Performance and Professional Supervisions

Professional supervision can help improve clinical areas of performance, and also staff morale, KPIs (Key Performance Indicators) regulated by external organisations like CQC/ local authorities, and other feedback, like customer reviews.

Effective supervision for staff can lead to better health outcomes for service users. It can also lead to aspects that improve management of the workforce: e.g. better attendance; less time off sick; better productivity; fewer mistakes; less grievances or complaints. This can lead to better feedback and ratings from service users, carers and even CQC.

How Performance Indicators can be used to Measure Practice

> The following clips provide a short introduction to the notion of key performance indicators:
> https://www.youtube.com/watch?v=9Co8slUvYj0
> https://www.youtube.com/watch?v=u_rmcItKfT8

Some examples of performance indicators could include:

- financial (budgets; spending levels);
- output (number of clients seen);
- impact (meeting standards;
- achievement of work objectives);
- reaction (customer feedback);
- time (response times; service delivery times)
- Some aspects of quality are better measured through qualitative forms of data – like concerns and complaints forms from service users.

The Problem of Power Imbalance and Professional Supervisions

It may feel that supervisions are being delivered for the best of intentions, and to support all parties, and interests of an organisation.

However, it must be remembered that they often don't 'feel that way' by employees themselves, especially by new members of staff.

The person conducting the supervision is usually in a managerial position with the potential ability to hire and fire, or issue disciplinaries. They may have a duty to monitor and report on matters like bad practice/ punctuality, and resolve conflicts.

There is therefore a power imbalance straight away. Sometimes there might be more of a positive kind of imbalance, because the supervisor might have more expertise or experience in the setting. On the other hand, there can also be an imbalance created by persona or body language. Some supervisors can be intimidating, whilst others can be more supportive.

Minimising Power Imbalances

If carried out well, observations are overwhelmingly very effective at improving working relationships between management and staff, and assisting performance management mechanisms. Done badly, however, and they can risk entrenching poor morale, and perceptions of management as being 'out of touch' or unaccountable.

These are many ways that can help address the power imbalance within professional supervisions. They are simple, but can be well worth implementing:

- Make sure the venue is quiet, friendly and private, so that the discussion can be confidential and not overheard
- Give the staff enough time to plan for the supervision, and make sure they know what time it will be and where it will be held.
- Make sure there will be enough time for the supervision, so they don't feel rushed or pressured.
- Make sure the discussions are constructive and solution-focussed.
- Set clear actions and target dates, and make sure there is accountability for whatever has been agreed.

Chapter 8: Ensuring positive outcomes for individuals

What is Outcome-based Practice

Traditionally, the quality of an organisation's performance, would be judged using measurements decided internally. These measurements would often tend to focus on outputs, such as to do with time, or expenditure.

However, outputs are very different to 'outcomes'. An organisation may have met their targets to deliver a service within budgetary limitations, or to increase clientele by a certain percentage in a given timescale. But the measurements against those targets, would still leave one none-the-wiser, as to the extent to which a service had helped individuals being looked after within that service, achieve their own personally-set outcomes[xix].

Focussing on outcomes set by service users themselves, helps to ensure that organisations are driven by the needs of their clientele, and not solely by financial or budgetary requirements. Moreover, one could also argue that being outcome-focussed, also helps to ensure that resources are deployed most effectively, and therefore can help to strengthen the underlying business model of the service.

There are different types of barriers to individuals achieving outcomes, personally expressed or aspired to.

These barriers may be:

- Environmental: The individual may live in a remote area and need support with transport in order engage with local communities. Alternatively, the individual might live in a congested urban conurbation, and require support to engage with busy transport hubs or to deal with local transport.

- Attitudinal/prejudicial: Some individuals may experience dampened down expectations, and not receive as much encouragement as others might receive, to maximise their opportunities, and to get the most out of them.

    For example, an older person with a physical disability, may be assumed to be 'too old' to want to maintain links with their local community and to be as physically active as possible.

    Alternatively, a person with learning disabilities with limited personal life experience, may not be encouraged to do certain things that are unfamiliar to them, and to limit their scope for development and to reach their full potential.

- Individual goals may vary widely, and some outcomes might be interpreted as being trivial to other people, but are important to that person. For example, the person might want to maintain their independence, and to be able to get in and out of bed on their own for as long as possible. Alternatively, maintaining a predictable routine, that makes them feel safe and secure, may be important to the individual, even though to the others this may seem quite unimportant. Sometimes attitudes towards other peoples' goals, or not encouraging them to be talked about or listened to, can also act as barriers to outcome-based practice.

Watch the following video clip from Helen Anderson Associates
on outcome-based practice:
https://www.youtube.com/watch?v=ZPfwORbJAs8

Different Approaches to Outcome-Based Practice

As we have seen, there are different sort of outcomes that may be important for service users or organisations.

These can be further divided into different types of outcomes[xx]:
- Outcomes involving change;
- Outcomes involving maintenance or prevention;
- And, service process outcomes.

According to a Knowledge Review carried out by the Social Care Institute for Excellence, organisations tend to focus on 'change' outcomes: for example, improvements in physical symptoms or behaviour, physical functioning and mobility, or morale.

However, individuals, especially older people, tend to place a higher value on outcomes that promote maintenance or prevention. These outcomes might include: feeling safe and secure; ensuring one's home is neat, tidy and clean; maintaining an active and alert mind; having social contact and companionship, with opportunities to help others; staying in control of everyday routines.

Service process outcomes are more about the experience of using the service, and might involve asking questions such as: did one feel valued and respected within one's care setting or service? Does the service user feel treated as an individual? To what extent are cultural and religious preferences respected and given space for expression?

One might say therefore, that the effectiveness of an outcomes-based approach, depends in part on the sort of outcomes one is focussing on.

An alternative approach was put forward by The Social Policy Research Unit (SPRU) in York[xxi], which builds on a framework that breaks down outcomes into a set of categories.

These outcomes include:

- **Autonomy outcomes:** e.g. being able to access all areas of one's home; having access to one's locality or wider environment; enjoying an adequate level of communicative access; having financial security.
- **Personal comfort outcomes:** e.g. personal hygiene; safety/ security; having desired level of cleanliness at home; emotional well-being; physical heath.
- **Economic participation outcomes**: e.g. having access to paid employment as required; having access to training; access to further/ higher education or employment; having access to appropriate training for skills.
- **Social participation outcomes**: e.g. access to mainstream leisure activities; having access to support in parenting role; access to support for personal secure relationships; access to advocacy/ peer support; citizenship.

This model is aimed much more towards younger disabled people, who need to have more broadly defined outcomes, and to receive support that is more flexible. The project conducted by the SPRU brought into relief the fact that service users found the outcome-focussed approach more useful than traditional needs-based approaches to assessment.

However, it was felt that social workers and practitioners found it difficult to adapt to new ways of working, and to see themselves as 'facilitators' rather than managers of budgetary targets and departmental requirements.

Outcome-Based Practice: Impact of Legislation and Policy Changes

The NHS and Community Care Act 1990	- Led to greater policy emphasis on outcome-based practice. Community care assessments became compulsory, with identification of individual needs. - Before that, assessment procedures were mainly resource-led: dependent on what resources were available, with very limited availability of services
1992: Community Care: Managing the Cascade of Change	- Led to increasing policy shift from service-led to needs-led approaches, with a proliferation in service providers in the health and social care market, dramatically increasing choice and competition.
2001: NHS Plan and National Service Framework for Older People	- Developed procedures for single shared assessments. - Placed emphasis on involving the service user in decision making. - The Fair Access to Care services (FACS) Guidelines (2003) developed, alongside the Single Assessment Process (SAP). This led to assessment of individual needs and risks. - Needs differentiated into four main categories: critical; substantial; moderate; low.

2014 Care Act	- Places statutory duty on local authorities to carry out assessment of anyone who appears to require care support, whether eligible for state-funded care. - Emphasis should be on outcome-based support, and prevention.

Impact on People's Lives: the Potential Benefit of Outcome-Based Practice

Outcome-based practice requires a much closer collaboration between social care practitioners and individuals in planning and assessment.

This dialogue and collaboration should be ongoing, and not limited to the initial assessment phase. It should continue from assessment planning, through to support planning and review.

When initial assessments of individual needs are more about checking 'eligibility criteria', then the process becomes more of a 'tick-boxing' exercise. The service user becomes more of a client, service user or patient: and less a citizen with rights and responsibilities.

Focussing on outcomes, can also lead to more preventative interventions becoming embedded in planning support. If an individual's priority is to 'feel connected with their family', then that person's family become a much more important part of that individual's care planning.

Needs-based assessment focusses generally on what an individual *cannot* do. Outcome-based practice focusses on what an individual *can do:* their strengths, capacities and goals.

By working with a focus on individual's outcomes and goals, you can tailor support so that it is delivered in such a way that it produces results that really matter to the person.

Consistent and committed focus on outcome-based practice, helps to ensure that individuals feel listened to, involved and respected.

This helps to reinforce a positive climate of open communication and transparency, that promotes safeguarding, control and personalised services.

The Psychological Basis for Well-being

Felicia Huppert has written extensively about this topic in her paper, 'Psychological Well-being: Evidence Regarding its Causes and Consequences' (2009)[xxii].

Huppert mentions that 'ill-being', or negative emotions, are a normal part of one's life: it is when they become extreme or long-lasting that they can interfere with an individual's ability to function in everyday life.

It might seem that 'feeling good' is everyone's chief goal. But in fact, 'functioning effectively' is probably more important. This includes: feeling interest, engagement, confidence and affection; having a sense of control and purpose; having positive relationships.

Some individuals have 'better chances' of 'feeling good' and functioning effectively emotionally. Those who have experienced parental warmth at early childhood, or have not experienced poverty, for example. Certain personality traits, such as positive styles of thinking or intrinsic motivation, also influence positive well-being.

Individuals who have not started off in life with societal advantages, can learn or be taught some of the traits that can influence well-being, at a population level – through therapeutic interventions, or education. It is possible to compensate for difficult beginnings.

Systems and Processes that Promote Individual Well-Being

What sort of support do you provide within your organisation, in the context of your role, to promote individual well-being? Think about the following dimensions, and describe how your organisation interprets or translates these ideas into practice in your own work setting:

- Holistic provision of care delivered through a multi-disciplinary team

- Comprehensive training and support provided to staff to underpin continuous professional development

- Awareness of safeguarding policies and procedures, and service users are encouraged to voice feelings and be heard.

- Understanding is promoted about how to encourage a balance between duty of care and supporting individuals to take risks.

- Staff are suppoorted to understand the social model of disability, and issues relating to this are discussed during supervisions or team meetings.

Promoting an Individual's Ability to have Choice and Control over their Decisions.

- Identify communication needs of service users;
- Develop positive attitudes within workforce in relation to equality and inclusion
- Promote a positive inclusive atmosphere and open climate of communication
- Encourage active participation
- Develop and promote an understanding of active support
- Support service users to make informed decisions: making information accessible and easy to understand
- Ensure you have a good understanding of the Mental Capacity Act 2015: all adults have a presumption of capacity: if an individual is deemed not to have capacity to make a certain decision, then the correct process must be followed.

Carers, Families and Significant Others: The Importance of Partnership Working.

Carers, family members and significant others often have expert knowledge and understanding of an individuals' needs.

They also have a legal right to be involved in the assessment process, as stipulated in the Care Act 2014. Carers also do a lot of work and support themselves, often for free. Their contribution is often much more valuable towards an individual's mental wellbeing, than other services.

It is important carers also receive advice and support on matters like: respite breaks; equipment; opportunities to obtain peer support or to mix with others in similar situations.

Sometimes carers can be vulnerable themselves: e.g. if they are looking after an individual who can exhibit challenging behaviour; or if they have care needs themselves.

Legislation that Promotes Partnership Working

The Care Act 2014 has introduced new rights and entitlements with regards to carers and families. Carers have an equal right in terms of assessment and support.

Social support services need to focus on well-being within the Care Act 2014 as well, and this means adopting more family-based approaches as well. They need to find ways and opportunities to integrate support for families better – not just for the individual who is being looked after.

Chapter 9: Safeguarding and protection of vulnerable adults

There is an important difference between the concept of safeguarding and the concept of protection in relation to vulnerable adults

Protection: 'Protecting' someone may at times feel quite close to *'controlling'* them. If somebody, perhaps a teacher, carer or parent, said to you right now that they wanted to 'protect you', would you feel safe and happy: or would you feel restricted, receiving an unwanted level of attention on your personal activities, and with a little less autonomy than you had before?

Protection is something that has a legal and moral basis within health and social care. It is a core tenet within the principle of duty of care, that individuals who are vulnerable for whatever reason, are protected from harm. It is important, however, that protection is balanced with another approach, which is *safeguarding.* What is safeguarding?

Safeguarding: The concept of safeguarding overlaps with protection, and does share a similar focus, in terms of helping to keep people safe. However, safeguarding also has a much wider meaning.

Safeguarding also includes:

- Ensuring and enabling individuals are able to take risks in a safe manner.
- Promote the principles of Positive Behavioural Support

- Helping to encourage and promote the right of individuals to be involved in risk assessment processes; to be involved in identifying, and agreeing how to respond to risks.
- Helping to ensure there is an emphasis on ***empowerment***[xxiii].

Safeguarding adults is about protection, justice and empowerment:

- Empowerment is about providing people with information and support to help them make informed choices, and informed consent.
- Protection is about keeping vulnerable individuals away from significant harm.
- Justice is about supporting these individuals to exercise their legal rights.

All of these principles are enshrined in the Human Rights Act 1998.

Approaches to Safeguarding in your own Setting: The Impact of Policy Developments

Within your work setting, analyse the role of the following to safeguarding:

- Safeguarding policies and procedures
- Risk management
- Personalisation
- DBS checks on new employees or applicants to roles within the setting

More recently, the following policy development has also impacted on safeguarding within work settings:

The Care Act 2014:

- The Care Act signalled in a number of important policy changes that affect the area of safeguarding
- The Care Act outlined Local Authority's responsibilities in regard to safeguarding within *primary legislation* (i.e. has become law)
- The Act also sets out that it is the local authority's primary responsibility to ensure enquiries into cases of abuse and neglect; to ensure the establishment of Safeguarding Adults Boards on a statutory footing, and with respect to information sharing.
- In certain circumstances, the Care Act also places a duty on local authorities to arrange independent advocacy to support

an adult or carer who is subject of an assessment, care or support planning or review.

Analyse the impact of this Act within your service setting: do you think there has been a significant impact?

Legislation Relating to Safeguarding of Vulnerable Adults[xxiv]

NHS and Community Act 1990	Outlined role of local authorities to assess people for social care and support, and to make sure those in need of community care services or other types of support, get the services they need and are entitled to.
The government paper, 'No Secrets'	Outlined how social services should promote collaborative working between multi-agencies to improve services to protect vulnerable adults from abuse.
Human Rights Act 1998	Ensures that interventions by the State into a person's life to protect them, strikes a balance that is proportional with their human rights. Interventions by the state must not be excessive, or impinge on their right to exercise autonomy and self-determination.
2007 'Putting People First'	This government paper outlined four key areas for improvement at council level: universal services; early interventions and prevention; choice and control and social capital.

Safeguarding Vulnerable Groups Act (2006)	Led to creation of the vetting and barring scheme and the Independent Safeguarding Authority.
Mental Capacity Act 2005	Outlines the principle that a person must be assumed to have capacity to make their own decisions, unless this can be proven to be otherwise. Even if this is the case, and the person does lack capacity, then intervention or support must be offered in the least restrictive way, and meet that person's best interests.
Care Standards Act 2000, and the setting up of the Care Quality Commission in 2010 under the Health and Social Care Act	Help to protect vulnerable adults in regulated residential settings.

Interrelationship of Serious Case Reviews and Safeguarding Processes

Serious Case Reviews are conducted when there has been a serious safeguarding issue, where an individual has lost their life or serious harm or abuse has occurred, and it needs to be investigated if service providers have failed in their duty of care. They provide a vital opportunity to make sure that services are held to account for any actions taken or not taken, and to scrutinise all the findings and relevant factors of a case, to elucidate lessons that can be learnt or identify ways to prevent the same mistakes being made again. If there is no serious case review, the chances are that the incident could happen again, and again.

Notwithstanding, there are some countervailing arguments as to the effectiveness of Serious Case Reviews. According to the Evidence Review in Adult Safeguarding, written by the Institute of Public Care in Feb '13, there are weaknesses to the current system of serious case reviews:

- There isn't a database available for the public to access reports carried out during Serious Case Reviews.
- It is not clear what the thresholds are which help to decide when a case is granted a Serious Case Review.
- Most cases that have invoked SCRs, involve older people (over the age of 60), and a third of these were resident in regulated settings, such as care homes. Fewer are carried out in relation to incidents that occur in unregulated settings.
- More research is needed to investigate the policy of adult safeguarding with respect to individuals with physical

disabilities, mental health conditions, women at risk of domestic violence, and forced marriage.
- There is little *evidence* to show that lessons identified from serious case reviews, are in fact used to improve work practice.

Notwithstanding, there are some prominent examples where Serious Case Reviews *have* had a positive impact on quality assurance, regulation and inspection:

- The Serious Case Review into the death of Stephen Hoskins, resulted in action on the part of Cornwall Council Adult Social Care Department to improve the risk assessment and review processes, to improve cooperation and partnership working between local, interagency vulnerable adult meetings; and ways to deal with safeguarding alerts in more sophisticated ways.[xxv]

- Following the scandal at Winterbourne View Hospital, the Department of Health's review lead to the better integration of safeguarding into primary legislation, in the form of the Care Act 2014.

What to do: Safeguarding Protocols and Referral Procedures

- Raise the alert! Notify your line manager, or Adult Social Care directly. Immediately if an emergency, or during same working day, or within four hours. Action must be taken to protect the adult at risk, and to ensure their immediate safety. If a criminal act has been suspected, then report the matter to the Police.
- Make a referral: this will be done usually by whoever has responsibility for safeguarding within your workplace. E.g. refer to Adult Social Care; Policy; CQC
- Strategy meeting involving the Safeguarding Adults Manager in Adult Social Care, with other professionals
- Investigation then takes place
- Risk management plan is then drawn up to ensure the safety of the individual concerned as well as others
- A case conference is convened
- A protection plan put in place, and reviews conducted to ensure that any actions agreed are followed

The safeguarding adults process can be closed at any stage if it is decided that an ongoing investigation isn't needed, or a protection plan has been agreed and implemented.

Chapter 10: Understand safeguarding of children and young people (for those working in the adult sector)

Policies, procedures and practices for safe working with children and young people

There are separate policies and procedures for safeguarding children and adults

Technically, the definition of a 'child' is someone who is under the age of 18.

Sometimes, however, services overlap. Some services provide for individuals with learning disability or autism, who may be over the age of 18, but are not able to live independently.

In addition, within the Children Act of 1989, there is an emphasis of the duty of care *of all organisations*, towards children, *even* services that provide support solely to 'adults'.

Calpin (2012) states that, in broad terms, the difference between adult and safeguarding is that 'there is a presumption of capacity in adults and a presumption of incapacity in children'.

Child Safeguarding: Legislative and Policy Guidelines

Every Child Matters (2003)	Followed the tragic death of Victoria Climbie. The Paper outlined five outcomes that should be strived for, in the context of well-being for all children and young people: - To be healthy - To be safe - To enjoy and achieve - To make a positive contribution - To achieve economic well-being. The paper also brought in the Common Assessment Framework, which was a scheme designed to standardise and make more consistent, the assessments that are made by social workers of children's needs.
Children Act 2004	Brought the five outcomes, outlined in the paper, Every Child Matters, into statute. The Act also brought about the setting up of Local Safeguarding Children Boards, and outlined the responsibility of different agencies and organisations to collaborate and cooperate on issues relating to child safeguarding. The Act also introduced

	the 'paramountcy principle': this means that the welfare of the child is paramount when making decisions about a child's upbringing, even for those working in adult services.
	The Children Acts of 2004 and 1989, were given further impetus by the Paper, 'Working Together to Safeguard Children'. This Paper further raised the awareness by practitioners of their responsibilities and duties by law.
Safeguarding Disabled Children Act (2009)	Brought in to provide additional protection for disabled children. Served to highlight the added vulnerability of disabled children.
The Children's Plan (2007)	Helped to define the role of the governments, and other agencies and professionals for improving the lives of children. Interlinked with the work of the **UN Convention on the Rights of the Child**, which was formally adopted by the UK in 1992.
The Sexual Offences Act 2003	Outlines what is considered as sexual offences, including forms involving physical and non-physical contact. Defines sexual offences against children under 13, and under 16, and

	sets the age of consent at 16 in most cases. Importantly, however, if an adult in in a position of trust in relation to a young person – for example, as their teacher, or care worker – then the age of consent is 18.
Care Act 2014	Includes some provisions for children and young carers. Young carers, under the Act, are entitled to an assessment to identify any support or help they need or require.
The Children and Families Act 2014	All carers under the age of 18 have the right to have their support needs assessed and local authorities must help them care for a family member as best as they can.

Child Safeguarding: Signs, Symptoms, Indicators and Behaviours

Physical abuse	- May be indicated by falls or minor injuries, that develop over time, and cannot be explained. There may be bruising that can't be explained in parts of the body that are quite well-protected, such as on the inside of the thighs or upper arms. - Bruising or injury that cannot be explained. - Unusual burn marks, e.g. cigarette burns. - Pattern of frequently changing GP; lack of willingness on part of children's family or guardians to attend appointments or cooperate with social or health professionals. - Malnutrition; being let in wet clothing. - Prescribed medicine that has not been administered.
Sexual abuse	- Unexplained, sudden or uncharacteristic changes in behaviour or withdrawal - Unusual expression of explicit sexual behaviour - Sudden or dramatic disturbances to sleep patterns - Bruising or bleeding in private areas - Torn or stained underclothing
Emotional abuse	- Loss of appetite or overeating; a state of anxiety or confusion; withdrawal or

	isolation - The child may have a heightened sense of fearfulness or low self-esteem - Pronounced disturbances in sleep patterns, or unusual displays of behaviour that is uncooperative or aggressive
Neglect	- Unkempt clothing or appearance - Sudden weight loss - Hasn't been given prescribed medication - Lack of adequate heating, lighting or food. - May not be allowed access to visitors, or contact with health or social care professionals
Radicalisation	- Where children have been taught extreme, sometimes violent, ideas linked to political, social or religious beliefs. - May exhibit behavioural changes; - Changing friendship circles; - Use of extremist terminology; - Reading extremist literature online
Child trafficking:	- Recruiting, moving or receiving a child through force, trickery or intimidation. - Signs and symptoms could include the presence of a domineering adult with a child, who doesn't let them speak. - The child may appear withdrawn, compliant and unkempt, with little English language.

Female genital mutilation (FGM):	- FGM is the removal, constriction or disfigurement of a girl's labia or clitoris for non-medical reasons. - Signs and symptoms include severe pain, bleeding, chronic infections, leading to psychological, mental health and sexual problems.

In Event of Allegations of Harm or Abuse by a Child

You should always act according to your internal organisational policies, and not go beyond the boundaries of your role.

Never personally investigate any allegations

If an allegation or disclosure has been made:

- Remain calm; give reassurance to the child, and *believe them*
- Listen very carefully, and do not interrupt or ask questions that are leading
- Do not promise to keep anything secret
- The priority should be on ensuring the child's safety
- Report any potential or actual abuse as soon as possible, to the NSPCC advice line, the local authority safeguarding advice line, or the Police.
- Collect any relevant and important information: including the date, time and location of the incident/ disclosure; the name, date of birth and address if known of the child; an impartial and factual account of the disclosure or allegation; an accurate and clear description of the injuries that were visible or present; a thorough recording of what immediate actions were taken, e.g. whether the police or an ambulance was called

Where Harm or Abuse is Suspected or Alleged: Rights of the Children, Young People and their Families

Children have the **right** to have their views **heard**, and to be able to express them in a way that is sensitive and age-appropriate.

This is in accordance to the UN Convention on the Rights of a Child (1989).

This **right** is also enshrined in the Human Rights Act (1998), which incorporates the European Convention on Human Rights into UK law.

Children also have a **right** to be kept safe, and that any allegations or witness of child abuse, are actioned upon as soon as possible.

In addition, children have a **right** to expect that information is shared between different relevant agencies, if necessary (e.g. Police, Health services and Local Authority)

Their families or carers, also have a **right** to be informed whenever harm or abuse has been alleged or suspected.

Chapter 11: Lead and manage group living for adults

Current theoretical approaches to group living provision for adults

There are three theoretical models that we will look at here, that are relevant to group living provision for adults:

Milieu Therapy	The theory of milieu therapy was developed by theorists, August Aichorn, Bruno Bettelheim, AS Neill, Melvyn Rose and Fritzl Redl.[xxvi]
	The word 'milieu' means 'environment'. The theory is underpinned by the principle that the environment should be seen as part of a therapeutic approaches experienced by service users. Service users often don't rely on short bursts of therapy, or therapy provided only by specialist professionals, but need the therapy to be embedded in the environment and setting around them.
	This is often especially true for individuals with behavioural difficulties.
	The aim is to shape a 'total' social environment.

	The environment encompasses an array of different aspects: such as the daily routine; opportunities for personal development; support to help individuals with relationship difficulties or with approaches to solve problems and dilemmas; strategies to help develop coping skills. The environment can also include aspects like the decoration and furnishings; are they warm and comforting, or cold and alienating; is there contact with animals and pets as part of the daily routine; is foot eaten together communally.
Systems Theory	Systems Theory sees human behaviour as multi-factorial: that it can be influenced by a variety of multiple multi-directional influences, sometimes at the same time, and at times in conflicting or contradictory patterns.[xxvii] Individual characteristics or personality traits are not influenced by internal factors alone, but a complicated array of internal and external factors, extending to families, organisations, societies and other co-existing systems.

Outcome based support	Outcome based support is about social care workers utilising formal and informal, regular and irregular opportunities with service users, to involve them in all aspects of their care, by helping to identify what they want their outcomes to be, what they are hoping to achieve, what is holding them back, and how they think they can get there.
	Service users are involved on a formal basis, once or twice a year, to review their care plan and to talk about anything that is concerning them. But they can also get involved in planning their day in the morning, or if an important event is coming up, or if there is a change in circumstances of some for.
	Local authorities need to be able to show or demonstrate, the impact and quality of the services provided, on individual outcomes.
	Underpinning this idea, is the principle that outcomes should be measured and monitored separately to outputs, such as 'hours worked', or 'expenditure'. Previously, the focus may have been on measuring the level of expenditure or hours of a service provided. The output may be a meal out of a particular care episode, but the outcome is improved social network, greater self-

| | esteem and confidence. |

Physical group living environments: legal and regulatory requirements

In the following section, is an overview of the legislation and regulations that are relevant to how a care provider should manage the physical group living environment of their care settings.

Safety:	- Health and Safety at Work Act 1974; - Management of Health and Safety at Work Regulations 2005
Care Quality:	- Care Act 2014; - Equality Act 2010
Protection of vulnerable people	- Safeguarding of Vulnerable Groups Act 2008; - Mental Capacity Act 2005; - Code of Conduct for Health and Social Care Workers.

There are a range of legal and regulatory implements that help to protect a minimum standard in care environments, and also in a more general way help to make sure that environments are safe both for the service users and the staff.

The Health and Safety at Work Act 1974, makes it a requirement that employers ensure that there is a safe workplace environment, and that suitable equipment is provided, together with training, to make sure that health and social care workers are able to do their job. Having the right equipment can be very important to ensure that service users with mobility problems, receive the correct support so they can manoeuvre as independently as possible in their surroundings.

The layout also needs to be considered, to make sure that there is sufficient space for ambulatory service users who can walk unaided, or with assistance. It's important that wheelchair users (particularly users of electric wheelchairs), have sufficient room to manoeuvre, as this not only promotes their sense of dignity, but reduces the risk of accidents or collisions between wheelchairs and ambulatory service users, visitors or staff.

The Care Act 2014 has helped to ensure that local authorities provide effective regulation, to make sure that services are outcome-focussed, that service users are involved in their care planning, and that wellbeing is treated with ultimate importance.

The Mental Capacity Act 2005 also has an impact on the physical group environment, as the MCA Act is about ensuring that service users with cognitive impairment, are involved in making decisions, and that carers do not remove from them the ability to make decisions just because of their disability. Also, the Act outlines how carers should act in their best interests, and use the least restrictive interventions.

This can have huge effects on a physical group living environment. For example, if an individual has a tendency to show challenging behaviour, this might upset other residents, who could also start shouting or getting aggressive. This could easily escalate, and lead to a situation where one of the service users might have to be taken to their room for a time to calm down, although this is potentially punitive, and could make the situation worse. It would be least restrictive and more proactive, to find ways to help someone manage their behaviour, or find ways to distract them or change focus earlier on, to avoid the challenging behaviour in the first place, and other service users getting upset as a result.

Maintaining the Right Balance: An Environment that is Safe and Secure, but also Promotes Freedom and Choice

Maintaining the right balance in an environment that is safe and secure on the one hand, but enables freedom and choice on the other, can be difficult but it is very important in order to address the needs of different service users, all with different needs.

Here are some examples of issues affecting this balancing act, and how to address them:

- Sometimes activities that a particular service user is doing, or enjoys doing, could pose a risk to other service users. For example, they might enjoy colouring, but other service users might use the pencils to throw or hurt someone.
    - So you could deal with this problem by making sure that the service users have the right staffing ratio, and that the other service users have activities to engage them too.
    - Or you could identify which service user is most at risk of throwing/ hurting himself, and organise the schedule so that he can do a different activity somewhere else at that time, or find somewhere safer for the other service users who do like colouring.

- Sometimes certain service users may not get on with each other, and are at risk of challenging behaviour or aggression when they are in the same room.
    - So you should try to address this difficulty, by organising the schedule so that they can use e.g. the kitchen or dining room at certain times when they will be on their own.

- You could find opportunities for them to try to share time with each other in small bursts and build it up, to try to help them develop a more positive relationship.
- You should make sure that all the service users are being treated equally and fairly, as sometimes service users may perceive 'preferential treatment', which can also exacerbate matters, and lead to potential conflict.

The Relationship between Physical Environment and Well Being

The physical environment can influence both one's mental and physical wellbeing in lots of ways.

The layout of an environment can influence service users' ability to mobilise freely to different areas of the setting. If they aren't able to access different areas of the setting, they can quickly feel 'trapped', or feel as if there are differential access rights in the setting.

Being able to mobilise freely can have a knock-on effect on your physical health. The more frequently and regularly that elderly service users can walk around, the easier it is to manage conditions like arthritis or stiff joints, and helps to prevent the risk of falls. Being as mobile as possible has equally beneficial effects for younger service users also, or those with mental health conditions or physical limitations.

The physical environment should be comfortable and homely, with areas where service users can put their own belongings, like their jacket and shoes, or favourite mug etc. These little things can help person feel as if they belong.

The environment should encourage service users to be individuals. If they enjoy music, there should be opportunities to listen to music whenever they want, or if they have a passion for football, it would be helpful if there were more than one television, to compromise between different tastes.

If the environment is plain, boring, with no personal belongings anywhere of the service users, and no obvious encouragement for freedom of movement or individuality, then this might be an indication of institutional abuse, which can have a hugely negative impact on someone's mental and physical wellbeing.

Link between Group Living and Positive Outcomes

Living in a shared environment, can help individuals to develop positive relationships and to develop their social and communication skills.

It enables them to develop a collective identity, and even develop friendship. There may be opportunities where they can help one another within the home, or have shared experiences together. They may learn a little bit about each other's backgrounds or individual differences, and develop a better understanding of individual uniqueness and the value of diversity.

Also, living in a shared environment can actually enable them to live with more independence than they might otherwise have been able to enjoy. For example, living on one's own can be more daunting for someone with disabilities, and there are more responsibilities. Living with others can enable everyone to 'pitch in', and to share the responsibilities, so they are as burdensome.
There are also some things that you can only do as a group, and you can't do on your own, such as play football or have a birthday party.

So group living can bring lots of opportunities to enhance a person's physical and mental wellbeing.

Chapter 12: Lead person-centred practice

What is Person-centred Practice?

Person centred practice is about putting the individual that is receiving support at the heart of all decision making and matters that affect them.

> Care and support should be *meaningful* to that individual, and focussed on individual values, preferences and needs.

> Individuals are not just 'objects' or passive recipients of care. Individuals have got biological, psychosocial and other very personal or practical needs, and all care should be holistic to take these into account.

> Person-centred practice is also about not creating an atmosphere of *risk aversion*, but rather developing understanding and systems for implementing positive risk management.

> Person-centred practice is about highlighting the rights and responsibilities of the individual as a citizen, focussing on their strengths, capacities and goals, and ensuring services do things *with* people, and not *at* them.

Approaches to Person-centred Practice

The following table gives an overview of a range of approaches to person-centred practice:

Personalisation	This approach is about placing the individual who receives support, at the heart of decision making, making choices that affect them, and in terms of identifying and prioritising needs. This approach is potentially transformative, but depends on the quality of information available to individuals, and the availability of advocacy and advice.
Biographical life-story work	This is about encouraging people to look at their life experiences in a biographical way. This can help individuals come to terms with traumatic times in their lives, but needs to be done sensitively, and at the individual's own pace – who may also need support and 'time-out', when they touch on painful or traumatic moments within their past.
Reablement	Reablement is about enhancing individuals' independent living skills, which also helps to increase confidence. This approach is more about helping an individual to regain skills, rather than to develop new skills. The approach is also more

	focussed on promoting independence, rather than resolving underlying health care issues.
Psychosocial interventions	This approach focusses on individuals wider social needs, that may be influencing or exacerbating an underlying psychological problem.

Person-centred Practice: Effect of Legislation and Policy

The following legislation all relevant in your analysis:

- Human Rights Act 1998
- Disability Discrimination Act 1995
- Equality Act 2010

Above, all intended to promote ability of disabled people to exercise their rights.

Better regulation:

- Health and Social Care Act 2010 – led to creation of Care Quality Commission

Legislation relating to consent:

- Mental Capacity Act 2005

The Health Foundation in 2012, sought to promote a cultural shift towards thinking that 'no decision about me, without me', needs to be central to all care settings.

Person-centred Practice and Establishing Consent

Consent is central to person-centred practice. It means that a person should not be given any type of medical treatment or examination, unless they have agreed to it. Consent should also be voluntary and informed.

This is also the case with regards to individuals who lack capacity to make decisions about their treatment.

The following link provides some further reading about assessing capacity: <http://www.hft.org.uk/Supporting-people/Family-carers/Resources/Using-the-Mental-Capacity-Act/>

If a major procedure is being planned, such as an operation, then there needs to be enough time between the establishing of consent and the procedure itself, to make sure that the individual has had enough opportunity to think everything through and ask questions.

Consent is part of a two-way discourse. The individual concerned should feel free and encouraged to ask questions, and express their views or feelings. It must be *informed consent.*

Some exceptions to this:

- If a child needs to undergo treatment, then the parent may be responsible for providing consent.
- End of life: if there is very little prospect of recovery of an individual, and the sole outcome of an intervention is to keep someone alive, and the person cannot express decisions

themselves, then an agreement can be reached between healthcare professionals, relatives and friends, to continue or stop that treatment.

The only times when consent is not necessary, is in the following circumstances:

- If the treatment is needed in an emergency, and the person lacks capacity at the time to give consent.
- If a person requires a life-saving procedure during an operation, then consent is not necessary.
- If a person has a severe mental health condition like dementia or schizophrenia, and does not have the capacity to provide consent, then consent again may not be necessary, although treatment of unrelated physical problems may still do.

Advance care planning:

- Person-centred practice is increasingly involving the use of 'living wills', also sometimes called advance directives. They are legally binding, and stipulate which sort of treatments or procedures an individual would refuse to have later in life, if at a time when they are unable to give informed and voluntary consent themselves.

Person-Centred Practice: Creating Positive Change in Individuals' Lives

Person-centred practice can have a positive impact on all the following aspects of individuals lives:
- Personal confidence and self-esteem
- Self-identity
- Relationships
- Trust in care staff and services
- More effective care planning
- Enhanced communication and self-advocacy skills
- Safeguarding

Chapter 13: Assess the individual in a health and social care setting

Assessment is about determining needs and, gauging what resources are available to meet those needs, while also weighing up the level of risk and urgency about the situation (Calpin et al, 2012)

Whittington ('07) defined the five purposes of assessment as:
- to protect the individual and the public
- to identify service user and carer needs
- to represent or advocate for the service users or carer
- to act on an agency's policies or priorities
- to inform other agencies or professionals

Sometimes assessments might be necessary due to a particular policy or initiative: for example, to promote the uptake of personal budgets.

Different forms of assessment are as follows:

Resource-led assessment	This is where the assessment is governed by the main priority to ration resources. It is not focussed on needs, but on what resources are available, and therefore limits users' influence and choice.
Needs-led assessment	This form of assessment focuses on individuals' situations, and what support and care needs are identified, and not

	what resources are available. This form of assessment does not have to focus on what individuals can't do, but also what they can do.
User-led assessment	This is a person-centred approach to assessment, whereby the user, or individual's views, are placed at the heart of decision making, and in terms of assessing needs and deciding how to address them. This approach is reflected in the words, 'No decisions about me, without me" (Coulter and Collins, '11)
Single assessment process (SAP)	The main purpose of this assessment tool was to help meet the needs of older people, by ensuring that professionals worked together when making assessments that affected older people. All older people who need to access support from social services, need to have an overview single assessment, which is carried out according to levels of risk, graded in terms of four levels – Low, Moderate, Substantial and Critical. Local councils have to provide support for anyone whose needs are either

	Substantial or Critical, and an annual review needs to take place to monitor all those assessed as either Low or Moderate.
Risk assessment	The purpose of this is to assess the level of risks and urgency posed by certain situations. However, their purpose is not just to keep people safe at all costs, but must also be person-centred, and bear in mind people's right to independence, choice and autonomy.

Partnership working: how this can positively influence assessment processes

Individuals who need support or care services, know best how their condition affects them.

Ensuring that they are at the centre of person-centred assessment processes, and in setting personal outcomes or objectives, leads to better services that are more responsive, and attuned to individual needs. (A Vision for Adult Social Care, DH, 2010).

Involving carers and families is also important, as they also often have an expert insight and understanding of the individual requiring support, and so councils should work with them in assessing needs. Carers and families also need to be part of the assessment process, to make sure that they also receive the care and support they receive, to have respite breaks, for example, or guidance and advice from carers organisations.

Personalisation means promoting the purchasing power and choice of individuals through the personal budget scheme, including direct payments. Increasing control in the hands of users and communities in this way, helps to support community-based organisations such as social enterprises, as well as universal service providers.

The aim of the government is to promote the plurality and diversity of services that individuals can access. This informs the assessment process as, along with ensuring individuals have adequate information about what services are available, they have many more choices relevant to their needs.

The increase in the diversity of services, helps to ensure that the assessment process is influenced less by the resource constraints of local authorities, and more by the needs expressed by individuals for preventative and other therapeutic services. The assessment process should also be about promoting choice, independence, with a focus on prevention and creativity of approach to addressing need.

Chapter 14: How to Respond to concerns and complaints

Managing Concerns and Complaints: Regulatory Requirements and Guidance

The Care Quality Commission, which was set up in 2009, is responsible for regulating the Health and Social Care Act 2008, which includes a provision regarding the handling of concerns and complaints.

The Code of Conduct, which is written by Skills for Care, also includes references to responsibilities in this regard.

Under Section 2, which governs the responsibility of social care workers to promote and uphold the privacy, dignity, rights, health and well-being of people, it includes the responsibility 'to always take comments and complaints seriously, respond to them in line with agreed ways of working and inform a senior member of staff'.

The Care Certificate, that was introduced in April 2015, and which has replaced the Common Induction Standards, also outlines the necessary training and understanding necessary by care workers in relation to handling concerns and complaints.

This includes the need to understand one's responsibilities in terms of handling comments and complaints in line with legislation and agreed ways of working, the need to ask for advice when necessary in dealing with them, and the need to understand the importance of learning from complaints in order to improve the quality of care service provided.

How Regulatory Requirements and Guidance Regarding Management of Concerns and Complaints affect own Service Provision

- What do you think are the pros and cons of the current regulatory requirements regarding concerns and complaints procedures, *in your own organisation*?
- Is there sufficient support for service users?
- Are service users familiar with the complaints procedure; would they feel at ease to utilise it?
- Do you monitor the number of concerns or complaints that are received, and the effectiveness of their handling?
- Are there areas of uncertainty in this area of policy? Are service users aware of their right to be able to complain?
- Is there support available for individuals who would need support to write a complaint, e.g. due to a disability or impairment?

Obstacles Experienced by Individuals when Raising or Making Complaints

Very few complaints are received each year. Some organisations receive 'no' complaints on a regular basis. This is a concerning area of health and social care, because given the vulnerability of people using health and support services, due to reasons of age, disability, illness or frailty, it is vital that there is a proactive stance to facilitate, encourage and support the exchange of views, concerns and indeed, complaints.

Complaints should not be seen as problems, or unwanted feedback. Quite the contrary, concerns and complaints are pivotal to ensuring a two-way flow of information from service users to management of service providers, without which there is no way that the effectiveness of services can be gauged, quality assessed or improvements planned or implemented.

Although at times challenging, receiving negative feedback in the form of concerns or complaints, forces organisations to think introspectively and respectively, and question or justify accepted ways of doing things. In other words, having an effectively system for concerns and complaints, helps to promote accountability.

To assess the effectiveness of your concerns and complaints procedures in your work setting, think about the following questions on the next page, all of which touch on different underlying reasons why service users might not raise a concern or complaint if they wanted to:

- Are individuals/ service users aware of their rights?
- Some service user may have experienced poor treatment in the past within other service providers. How can they be supported to be aware of their rights, and feel empowered to raise concerns should they feel they need to?
- There may be physiological reason that makes it hard to complaint: e.g. difficulties with speech (e.g. dysarthria); difficulty to write (e.g. due to stroke; dyslexia). What sort of support is provided to people who struggle to communicate?
- Is there access to independent advocacy to support individuals who wish to make a concern or complaint?
- Are they fearful of being seen as a 'trouble-maker', or fearful of being harassed, targeted or discriminated as a result?
- Some service users might be wary of upsetting family members who have helped find them their current placement, or if they have care needs of their own. What support mechanisms are in place?
- If they are very dependent on their carer, they will be fearful of not being able to meet their own care needs, if they were to raise a complaint against staff who are supporting them. How are service users empowered and supported to feel able to exercise their rights?

How to Encourage and Empower Individuals to use Complaints Mechanisms to Make their Voice Heard

Consider the following aspects:

Promote an open culture of communication, tolerance and accountability
Facilitate open dialogues; involving service users in reviews; giving opportunities as regularly as possible to give feedback and be involved in shaping of the service
Ensure there is accessible information relating to complaints procedures
Remember that individuals can make complaints in lots of different ways: e.g. verbally; over the phone; by email; or by letter; or through an advocate or an online feedback form.
Respect individual's confidentiality: assure them that any concerns will be treated with utmost confidence according to Caldicott Principles and Confidentiality Policy
Respond to complaints promptly; take them seriously and demonstrate a commitment to continuously improving practice.

Apply and Demonstrate

Show how you have assisted in the development of procedures to deal with concerns and complaints:

- Review complaints policy and procedures following feedback from service users, other stakeholders and staff
- Consult on any changes needed through team meetings or management meetings
- Update communication plans and individual support plans
- Get up-to-date information from organisations such as CQC or ACAS to relay to staff and service users.

Make sure information about complaints procedures is accessible.
Consider the following aspects:

- Provide leaflets in accessible format or different language formats.
- Utilise resources from BILD (British Institute for Learning Disabilities)
- Mention relevant information orally during service users' reviews.

Show that you are able to assess, monitor and review complaints mechanisms:

- What has gone well in terms of changes recently implemented?
- What improvements are still to be made?

Chapter 15: Facilitate change in health and social care or children and young people's setting

Factors that drive change

There is a wide array of factors that influence systems and change processes. Some factors that drive change within an organisation originate internally, others externally. The following table analyses these dynamics a little more closely. Try to think of how these issues may relate to your own organisation, or if you can think of other drivers for change that are pertinent.

Work environment	For example: - What sort of care setting is it? - Is it an old or modern, purpose-built building? - Are there surrounding facilities, such as garden space or communal areas? - Is it in proximity to countryside, or is it in a busy urban conurbation?
Processes	- How are decisions made? - Who has responsibility or capability to facilitate or enable change?
Workplace culture	- How supported do employees feel within the workplace?

	- Do they feel valued or treated equally?
Relationships/ behaviours	- Do employees support one another, or is there a climate of competition and mutual distrust? - Relationships can also be influenced by different types of personalities that make up teams, and the different kinds of skills and abilities of different employees.
Style of leadership	- Is the style of leadership *transactional*, which means being chiefly characterised by issuing of commands and instructions, or: - *Transformational*, which is about seeking to involve others and generate a sense of ownership and belonging within the organisation.
Effective planning and decision-making	- Having a clear understanding of what the outcome of change is intended to be; - Breaking down a plan into clear achievable and measurable steps
Effective communication	- Effective communication; involvement of all staff and stakeholders

All of the above factors also influence the drive for change. Change management requires managers or leaders to understand all these aspects to a setting. 'Change management' produces nothing if it is simply 'imposed' on a setting, without consultation with others. Effective change management, is where change happens, because they are implemented comprehensively, effectively and seamlessly, and the lasting benefits of change are achieved.

For more information about this, go to the following links:
http://www.mindtools.com/pages/article/newPPM_87.htm

http://www.businessballs.com/changemanagement.htm

Underpinning theories of change management

Two widely known theories of change management are that of the 'Change Curve', and 'Psychological Contract' theory.

For more information about these and other theories, you can go to the links shown below, but a short summary of these two theories will be outlined below:
- http://www.mindtools.com/pages/article/newPPM_96.htm
- http://www.businessballs.com/psychological-contracts-theory.htm

The **'Change Curve'**:

- Is a widely used model often applied to change management processes, or adapted for different contexts.
- The model is often attributed to Elisabeth Kubler-Ross, a psychiatrist who studied about the personal transitions during the emotions of grief and bereavement.[xxviii]
- There are four stages that people have to go through during the process of adjusting to change.
    - During the first stage, which is when change is introduced, the initial reaction is shock or denial.
    - Stage Two, is when negative reactions or emotions to the change come to the fore – people may be fearful, angry or actively resist or protest against the changes. At this stage, chaos could ensure if the situation isn't managed carefully.

- o The Third Stage of the change curve, is when people start to accept the changes and start to consider ways of adapting to the change.
- o Stage Four is when people have accepted and even begun to embrace the changes. During this phase, it is the important that managers or leaders try to minimize the negative impact of change as much as possible, and help people adapt to change more quickly by giving them the information and help they need.

The '*Psychological Contract' theory*[xxix]:

- Is also often used to help understand change management, and is a theory that was developed in the 1960s by the organisational and behavioural theorists Chris Argyris and Edgar Eschein, although it has been contributed to since as well.
- It is sometimes represented diagrammatically using the *'psychological contracts iceberg model'*.
- The metaphor of an iceberg is used because only a tip of an iceberg is seen from the surface, the rest being hidden or submerged.
- In the context of employee-employer relationship, the elements that might be 'seen' are written contracts, but there is also an intangible 'psychological contract' that is built up of the mutual expectations between employer and employees, of inputs and outcomes, or 'what the employee puts into the job', and 'how the employee is treated by the employer'.
- External pressures form the market, which influence output or pay levels, can push the iceberg down, so more becomes submerged.

- The greater the clarity, depth and visibility of the psychological contract, the more the 'contract value and written contractual expectations start to risk, and the 'iceberg' becomes more visible above the water line.
- Put in simple terms, when trying to implement change, managers and leaders should find opportunities to encourage better communication, understanding and agreement of intangible mutual expectations with employees, which help promote trust and understanding, far more than the 'contract of employment' alone.

Supporting the Change Process: Approaches, Tools and Techniques

> Go to the following link, to research more about this topic:
>
> http://www.businessballs.com/consciouscompetencelearningmodel.htm

John P. Kotter believed there were 'eight steps to successful change'. He wrote about them in his book, 'Leading Change' (1995). They are a useful structure or toll to help guide the change process[xxx].

Stage 1	First of all, it is necessary to 'increase urgency', which means the process by which people are inspired to develop ideas or suggestions for change.
Stage 2	Then, it is necessary to 'build the guiding team', which involves making sure people with equal levels of emotional commitment, skills and attributes can help initiate the change.
Stage 3	The third stage is to 'get the vision right'. This means communicating the vision, strategies and

	values behind the proposed change. In the context of health and social care, communicating the values is very important, and making sure they are reinforced and everyone feels inspired and committed to them.
Stage 4	'Communicating for buy-in', is described by Kotter as the process by which people are persuaded to get actively involved.
Stage 5	The fifth stage is where leaders work proactively to remove the obstacles, giving lots of support, feedback, encouragement and praise, which all help to 'empower action'.
Stage 6	In this process, it is necessary to make people feel they are achieving along the way, and so leaders need to make aims achievable – 'short-term wins'.
Stage 7	In this process, it is necessary to make people feel they are achieving along the way, and so leaders need to make aims achievable – 'short-term wins'. Kotter then describes the seventh stage as 'don't let up' – encourage motivation through monitoring and review of progress, and giving

	lots of encouragement.
Stage 8	The final stage is 'make change stick', by which change is gradually embedded and interwoven into culture, and the values of the change are reinforced through recruitment processes, promotion and new change leaders.

Other tools that can help to facilitate the change process:

- Brain-storming sessions: can be facilitated through workshops or team meetings; helps to generate a sense of involvement and mission; helps to develop a sense of ownership or buy-in into the change processes.
- Staff surveys: helps to identify where change is needed; priorities perceived by staff; helps to promote engagement and sense of being valued.
- Time: it is important that change isn't brought about too quickly, and without first promoting communication at the outset, and participation and involvement of all those who will be affected by the change.

'Conscious competence theory[xxxi]':

- This theory is often attributed to the US organisation, Gordon Training International. It helps to emphasise the importance of not rushing change.
- In the process of learning and training, at the start the learners are at the stage of 'unconscious incompetence'.
- As training progress and understanding deepens, together with an ability to apply to work practice, they go through the other three stages, which are: conscious incompetence; conscious competence and 'unconscious competence'.

The model serves to emphasise how important it is for trainers and tutors not to wrongly assume trainees are at Stage 2, and to rush them on to the next stage, when actually they are still at Stage 1.

The theory argues that learners will not be able to achieve conscious competence, unless they are fully aware and conscious of their incompetence before. It is argued that 'this is a fundamental reason for the failure of a lot of training and teaching'.

Apply and Demonstrate

As part of the Level 5 Diploma, you will need to show and demonstrate how you implement the concepts and principles of change management, to your own workplace setting:

- What has gone well in terms of changes recently implemented?
- What improvements are still to be made?
- When will a review of the policy be next made?
- Are there regular reports collated (e.g. annually) for analysing complaints received, and for ensuring that lessons are learned?

Chapter 16: Explore Models of Disability

Models of Disability

There are two main models of disability that mostly dominates discussion of this topic. These will be described first, although there are other models that will be described later as well[xxxii].

The Medical Model of Disability	Within this model, the focus is on the 'impairment' or whatever has caused a problem or illness for a person: e.g. disease; trauma; other health condition.
	The perspective of clinically trained professionals predominates;
	An emphasis is placed on finding a 'cure', or to create enough improvement in the individual's condition or behavioural state, that there is almost a cure.
	In terms of care and treatment, an emphasis is placed on the importance of medicines and drugs, and prescribed interventions.
The Social Model of Disability	In contrast to the medical model, this model sees disability as less a medically defined problem or deficiency, but more a socially-created problem.

	The model also sees disability as arising from a multitude of different factors, including biological (i.e. the condition), but also social or environmental.
	By altering or removing obstacles in the environment, carers can go a long way towards alleviating some of the negative effects of having a disability.
	Implicit in this model, is also the notion that attitudinal barriers or prejudices towards people with disabilities also goes a long way to explaining why there are obstacles and impediments to disabled people in the environment in the first place.
	By discussing and breaking down some of these prejudices, we can create a larger body of understanding and proactive energy to improving the environment and social context in which disabled people find themselves.
The Expert or Professional Model of Disability	This model is similar to the medical model. Within this model, an emphasis is placed on the role of professionals to identify the impairment and its effects, and to manage the recommendation and implementation of interventions.
	Overall this model creates an impression of an

	authoritarian, over-active care provider: while the service user is seen as passive and 'incapable'.
The Tragedy and/or Charity Model of Disability	Within this model, disabled people are seen as tragic figures, who should receive pity, and are seen as weak and dependent on others.
The Empowering Model of Disability	This model places an importance on the individual, and his/ her family, being able to be involved in their care and treatment, and decisions about what services to utilise and access.
	The model causes a shift in the role of the professional to that of 'service provider' or facilitator, whose role is to provide advice and guidance, find out the service user's wishes, and to empower them or facilitate their wishes, preferences and goals.
The Economic Model of Disability	This model focuses on the economic implications and effects of disability, in particular the person's inability to work.
	The model also looks at the extent to which a person's productivity is affected by their impairment, and the wider economic consequences of their impairment, such as increased benefit requirements, loss of

	earnings, financial hardship.
	The model is also related to a certain degree with the charity/ tragedy model.
The Market Model of Disability	This model focuses on the consumer needs and importance of disabled people as a group, and sees disabled people as consumers, employees and potentially voters, who governments need to be aware of and make sure their needs are addressed.

Different Models of Disability: How they are Experienced

Service users may experience different perspectives on disability depending on who they are talking to, or the context of their care.

If they are in a hospital, they may find that the medical model predominates. If they are living in their own home, supported by domiciliary carers, they may find that the social care model is more pronounced.

- They also may experience different perspectives and approaches towards disability based on who they are talking to. If they are talking to family members or friends, they may demonstrate the social model more. However, when talking to a medical professional like a doctor or nurse, they may find that the medical model is brought to relief. When talking to unfamiliar people or people in the public, they may experience the tragedy/ or charity model of disability.

- These are generalisations, and there are variations of course in terms of attitudes towards disability on an individual basis, and also in terms of culture. Some cultures may be more positive towards disability issues than others.

Different Models of Disability: Effect on Organisational Structures and Outcomes

- In clinical settings, such as hospitals or medical centres, there is an emphasis on the medical model of disability, because clinical professionals have tended to have focused their training on the medical dimensions of a condition more than the environmental or societal aspects that can also impact on a person's quality of life. Some organisations, such as 'Autism Speaks' campaign energetically for funding and donations to contribute towards ongoing research and treatment options. For many, the medical model isn't necessarily a 'negative model' at all.

- Social care organisations may focus more on the social model of disability however, as in community settings, clients are often being supported who have long-term conditions, and have no real prospect of being 'cured', and the focus of professionals is to promote their quality of life with as broad a range of activities and stimulation as possible.

- Sometimes people with physical or mental disabilities may also find themselves living in the community, and they do not want to discard the life they had before or aspire to have, but want to be as independent as possible and to fulfil as many aspirations as they can in life.

- User-led organisations or independent charities are often more helpful to such individuals and their families, and are structured to be less formal, and more inclusive of people, valuing their individuality and diversity.

Apply and Demonstrate

Show how agreed ways of working in your own work setting can help promote certain models of disability:

- What aspects of your organisation represent the 'medical' and 'social' models of disability?
- E.g. doctors; psychiatrists; consultants – probably more the 'medical' model?
- Occupational therapists; speech and language therapists; support workers; family members; friends – probably more the 'social' model?
- Agreed ways of working, means what processes or procedures influence either of these models: e.g. medical reviews; team meetings; residents' meetings; multi-disciplinary teams.

What would you recommend to improve involvement and empower the service users in your care?

For example:

- Involve them more in discussions about how well they feel supported; do they have any goals or aspirations that are currently unfulfilled or unsupported?
- What is working in the current environment or setting, and what's not working?
- Do they find approaches of staff friendly and helpful?
- You could ask staff to reflect on their approaches, to

Apply and Demonstrate

Implement actions to carry out recommendations:
- Write a reflective account describing what you did to implement the changes you recommended, or decided needed to be done, to improve empowerment and participation.

Promote awareness and understanding of other staff of models of disability
For example:
- Discussion of these areas during supervision
- You could deliver a short training session during staff handover, or during a team meeting
- You could put up some posters in staffroom areas to raise awareness about models of disability
- Make available e-learning or other forms of learning that staff could undertake independently
- ..... what else can you think of? Think of your own ideas, or how you could implement the above in your own setting.

Show how you implemented these activities
Demonstrate how you reviewed the outcome these activities:
- What went well in terms of the actions you implemented above?
- What didn't go well?
- What did you learn from the process?
- What would you do differently next time?

References

[i] Anon, Communication Quotes. *BrainyQuote*. Available at: https://www.brainyquote.com/topics/communication [Accessed 2019].

[ii] Crook M. A. (2003). The Caldicott report and patient confidentiality. *Journal of clinical pathology*, *56*(6), 426-8.

[iii] Burgess, M., 2019. What is GDPR? The summary guide to GDPR compliance in the UK. *WIRED*. Available at: https://www.wired.co.uk/article/what-is-gdpr-uk-eu-legislation-compliance-summary-fines-2018 [Accessed 2019].

[iv] Anon, *Effective supervision*. Available at: https://www.skillsforcare.org.uk/About/What-we-do/Workforce-development-strategy.aspx [2019].

[v] Mcleod, S., 2017. Kolb's Learning Styles and Experiential Learning Cycle. *Simply Psychology*. Available at: https://www.simplypsychology.org/learning-kolb.html [Accessed 2019].

[vi] Anon, Gibbs' Reflective Cycle. Helping People Learn From Experience. *Groupthink - Decision Making Skills Training from MindTools.com*. Available at: https://www.mindtools.com/pages/article/reflective-cycle.htm [Accessed 2019].

[vii] Anon, Skills for Learning. *Example 1 - Kolb's Learning Cycle | Models for structuring reflection | Skills for Learning Preview*. Available at: https://skillsforlearning.leedsbeckett.ac.uk/preview/content/models/04.shtml [Accessed 2019].

[viii] Anon, Available at: https://www.skillsforcare.org.uk/Learning-development/inducting-staff/care-certificate/Care-Certificate-workbook.aspx [Accessed 2019].

[ix] Anon, *NHS Choices*. Available at: https://www.nhs.uk/conditions/consent-to-treatment/ [Accessed 2019].

[x] Anon, Using the Mental Capacity Act. *Social Care Institute for Excellence*. Available at: https://www.scie.org.uk/mca/introduction/using-mental-capacity-act [Accessed 2019].

[xi] Anon, At a glance 31: Enabling risk, ensuring safety: Self-directed support and personal budgets. *Social Care Institute for Excellence*. Available at: https://www.scie.org.uk/publications/ataglance/ataglance31.asp [Accessed

2019].

[xii] Anon, Forming, Storming, Norming, and Performing - Understanding the Stages of Team Formation. *Groupthink - Decision Making Skills Training from MindTools.com*. Available at: https://www.mindtools.com/pages/article/newLDR_86.htm [Accessed February 2019].

[xiii] Anon, Leadership Styles Choosing the Right Approach for the Situation. *Groupthink - Decision Making Skills Training from MindTools.com*. Available at: https://www.mindtools.com/pages/article/newLDR_84.htm [Accessed 2019].

[xiv] Calpin, P.J., 2012. *Diploma in leadership for health and social care*, Cheltenham: Nelson Thornes.

[xv] Anon, The Nine Belbin Team Roles. *Belbin*. Available at: https://www.belbin.com/about/belbin-team-roles/ [Accessed 2019].

[xvi] Anon, 2019. Martin Seligman. *Wikipedia*. Available at: https://en.wikipedia.org/wiki/Martin_Seligman [Accessed 2019].

[xvii] Phil, Performance Management Cycle. *The Happy Manager*. Available at: https://the-happy-manager.com/articles/performance-management-cycle/ [Accessed 2019].

[xviii] Calpin, P.J., 2012. *Diploma in leadership for health and social care*, Cheltenham: Nelson Thornes, p.122-3

[xix] Anon, HSA | Person-centred | Personalisation | Training | Consultancy. *Helen Sanderson Associates*. Available at: http://helensandersonassociates.co.uk/ [Accessed 2019].

[xx] Anon, SCIE Knowledge review 13: Outcomes-focused services for older people. *Social Care Institute for Excellence*. Available at: https://www.scie.org.uk/publications/knowledgereviews/kr13.asp [Accessed 2019].

[xxi] University of York, Publications. Available at: https://www.york.ac.uk/spru/publications/ [Accessed 2019].

[xxii] Huppert, F.A., 2009. Psychological Well-being: Evidence Regarding its Causes and Consequences. *Applied Psychology: Health and Well-Being*, 1(2), pp.137–164.

[xxiii] Anon, At a glance 31: Enabling risk, ensuring safety: Self-directed support and personal budgets. *Social Care Institute for Excellence*. Available at: https://www.scie.org.uk/publications/ataglance/ataglance31.asp [Accessed 2019].

[xxiv] Anon, Available at: https://www.skillsforcare.org.uk/Learning-development/inducting-staff/care-certificate/Care-Certificate-workbook.aspx [Accessed 2019].

[xxv] Anon, Safeguarding adults: lessons from the murder of Steven Hoskin. *Social Care Institute for Excellence*. Available at: https://www.scie.org.uk/socialcaretv/video-player.asp?guid=55e3a233-c880-4cb4-8701-4acb9d243d39 [Accessed 2019].

[xxvi] Anon, What Is Milieu Therapy And Why Is It Used? *Regain*. Available at: https://www.regain.us/advice/therapist/what-is-milieu-therapy-and-why-is-it-used/ [Accessed 2019].

[xxvii] Anon, GoodTherapy.org. *GoodTherapy.org - Find the Right Therapist*. Available at: https://www.goodtherapy.org/learn-about-therapy/types/systems-theory-therapy [Accessed 2019].

[xxviii] Anon, Kubler-Ross Five Stage Model. *Change Management Coach*. Available at: https://www.change-management-coach.com/kubler-ross.html [Accessed 2019].

[xxix] Anon, Home. *Course: Free Online Improving Workplace Performance Training*. Available at: https://www.businessballs.com/building-relationships/the-psychological-contract/ [Accessed 2019].

[xxx] Webster, V. & Webster, M., 2017. Successful Change Management - Kotter's 8-Step Change Model. *Leadership Thoughts*. Available at: https://www.leadershipthoughts.com/kotters-8-step-change-model/ [Accessed 2019].

[xxxi] Anon, Home. *Course: Free Online Improving Workplace Performance Training*. Available at: https://www.businessballs.com/self-awareness/conscious-competence-learning-model/ [Accessed 2019].

[xxxii] Disabled World, 2017. Definitions of The Models of Disability. *Disabled World*. Available at: https://www.disabled-world.com/definitions/disability-models.php [Accessed 2019].

Printed in Great
Britain
by Amazon